Praise for *How to Lead Your Family Business*

"Julie Charlestein's leadership is authentic and effective—traversing the landscape of business in a personal, relatable, and successful way. Her lessons will serve to help other leaders as they engage and develop their organizations."
— Stanley Bergman, Chairman and CEO of Henry Schein,
Inc. 2017 Chief Executive of the Year

"*How to Lead Your Family Business* is a must-read for any entrepreneur who must journey through the challenges of relationships and draw on their full intellectual, experiential, and emotional abilities."
—Gil Bashe, Chair of Global Health and Purpose at Finn Partners

"Leadership through engaging and energized storytelling is what Julie Charlestein delivers. Relaying valuable insights and actionable strategies, *How to Lead Your Family Business* is the guide for executives, entrepreneurs, and business owners. Plus, who can resist *My Cousin Vinny?*"
—Mark S. Wolff, DDS, PhD, Morton Amsterdam Dean,
University of Pennsylvania School of Dental Medicine

"Julie Charlestein well understands the opportunities and challenges of leading and growing a family business. In *How to Lead Your Family Business*, Charlestein provides actionable guidance for family business owners and leaders through insightful and humorous vignettes, making it a must-read for anyone working in a multigenerational family business."
—Bill Rock, President of MLR Holdings and
Publisher of *Family Business* magazine

"Before I read this book, I already knew that my cousin Julie was a brilliant leader who had expertly guided our family's business through times of both growth and crisis. But what I did *not* know was that she is also a killer writer, capable of chronicling Premier's (and our family's) ups and downs with razor-sharp wit, priceless wisdom, and, of course, laugh-out-loud humor. (I can't believe the whole world will now know all about our grandmother's elaborate 1970s computer-dating scheme.) This book is as enjoyable to read as it is valuable in its expertise."

—Amy Phillips, Managing Editor of Pitchfork

"Brilliant! This book is sure to inspire those contemplating going into their family's business and certain to entertain those who aren't. Julie Charlestein has captured the true struggle that all successful multigenerational family businesses face and shared these struggles with humility, honesty, and wit. As an owner and former CEO of a 107-year-old family business, you can't make this stuff up. Julie's intent and intellect have made her into the amazing leader she is today and will continue to be."

—Anne Eiting Klamar, MD, Chair of the Board, Midmark

How to
Lead
Your
Family
Business

How to **Lead** Your **Family Business**

Excelling Through Unexpected Crises, Choices, and Challenges

JULIE CHARLESTEIN

Matt Holt Books
An Imprint of BenBella Books, Inc.
Dallas, TX

Matt Holt is an imprint of BenBella Books, Inc.
10440 N. Central Expressway
Suite 800
Dallas, TX 75231
benbellabooks.com
Send feedback to feedback@benbellabooks.com.

BenBella and *Matt Holt* are federally registered trademarks.

Printed in the United States of America
10 9 8 7 6 5 4 3 2 1

Library of Congress Control Number: 2022033489
ISBN 9781637742792 (hardcover)
ISBN 9781637742808 (electronic)

Editing by Katie Dickman
Copyediting by Alyn Wallace
Proofreading by Jenny Rosen and Madeline Grigg
Text design and composition by Jordan Koluch
Cover design by Paul McCarthy
Printed by Lake Book Manufacturing

Dedicated to Gram and Grandpa, who gave me everything.
Abba, who taught me everything.
And "The Suck It Crew," who are my everything.

Contents

Introduction

Welcome (and I Use That Word Carefully)
to the Family Business

We've probably been in your mouth.

I'm the CEO of Premier Dental Products, a company you've most likely never heard of. But, like I said, we've probably been in your mouth. The products we sell are used in more than seventy-five countries around the world and include such popular items as Traxodent® hemostatic and retraction paste (which displaces soft tissue around your damaged tooth), the Triple Tray® (the plastic gadget your dentist uses to take an accurate impression of your teeth when preparing a crown or bridge), and Enamel Pro® prophy paste (which your dental hygienist uses when polishing your teeth to give you that fresh, straight-from-the-dentist feeling).

Trust and believe, I could go on and on about what makes these and other Premier products the most phenomenal things ever. But I can tell you're already over it. Let's just say that Premier is a name your dentist is probably very familiar with and trusts implicitly on a daily basis. Which means that, again without your knowing it, Premier has probably taken care of you.

Business relationships don't get much more intimate than that.

Premier was founded in 1913 by a dental instrument sharpener named Julius Charlestein, and the similarity of our names is no coincidence. Julius was my great-grandfather, and I am the fourth-generation member of the Charlestein family to run the company. Which means that, yes, I am a grateful beneficiary of that old business tradition known as nepotism. Like many of America's most successful companies, from Mars, Incorporated (the candy people) and News Corp to Ford and Walmart, Premier is a family business, and my career story simply wouldn't be the same if I hadn't been born a Charlestein. It's a privilege to be part of a family that has nurtured an outstanding company over four generations and to inherit the values, traditions, and opportunities it has created. I never forget that fact.

On the other hand, it would be a mistake to assume that my leadership journey has been a smooth and easy one. Quite the opposite. My family is a fun-loving and lively bunch of people whose occasional dysfunctions (including my own) are part of the charm.

Family dramas can be the most intense dramas of all. (Have you seen the Giudices and the Gorgas on *The Real Housewives of New Jersey*? You'll come to learn through this book that I am obsessed with all reality TV—especially on Bravo.) And being in business together doesn't make those family dramas any simpler.

Getting back to nepotism . . . I'm sure some people in family businesses might try to take advantage of it, figuring that power and money will flow their way automatically. Not my jam. (Though sometimes I wish it *was!*) If anything, I've always felt an intense pressure to prove myself—to earn my reputation and to demonstrate that I have what it takes to lead the company my family created and not to be the one that fucks it up.

The person I particularly wouldn't want to disappoint is my grandfather, Morton Charlestein—or Mr. M., as he was affectionately known by those at Premier. Grandpa was just the best—wise, humble, gentle yet tenacious—and he established values and leadership principles that I strive to embody. He made Premier into a company that is universally respected throughout our industry, and his insightful sayings—lovingly referred to as "Mortonisms"—are frequently quoted by leaders not just at Premier but in the industry overall. (I'll be citing them throughout this book.)

So I've always been acutely conscious of the expectations that go with my name. Some people at Premier and in our broader industry expected that I would rise to the challenge. A few expected that I would fail—and a couple may even have looked forward to watching that happen. But the external pressures I felt were nothing compared to the internal pressures that I created for myself.

I hadn't planned to follow my grandfather and my father into the executive suite at Premier. While in college, I launched an independent career in news media, interning for two years at CNN. Later I was a legislative assistant for the American Israel Public Affairs Committee (AIPAC). That didn't end well, as I'll explain in a bit.

I finally joined Premier full time in 2003, after I'd earned my master's degree in business from Temple University, worked in the telecom industry at RCN Corporation, and gotten pregnant with my first child, my daughter Ruby. By then, I'd developed an array of talents, skills, and knowledge through years of work and business education. When I joined "the business," I started out as one of Premier's product managers, a good perch from which to learn the intricacies of our company and of the dental industry overall. My father, Gary Charlestein, was then the CEO of Premier.

I knew I had a lot to prove—and a lot to learn. Though some of what I had to learn I didn't even realize. For example, I didn't anticipate how embroiling it would be to work with my father. Most of my learning came through on-the-job experience, many times with pains and frustrations attached.

After I'd been in the business for a year or two, I realized that I needed to understand much more about how our own organization was structured. How would leadership transitions be handled? What plans were in place for long-term succession? What are various tax implications and structures? I was becoming increasingly engaged in thinking about the future of Premier, and I could see that the answers to questions like these would have a huge impact on that future.

I asked to see the documents governing these matters. (That kind of access is one of the privileges you get when you're one of the family.) Well, they were somewhat vague, confusing, and lacking. Of course, they were legal documents, so there's that. They reflected Premier's century-old origins as a family enterprise, like many family businesses in which major decisions were handled informally, via dinner-table conversations—a not-uncommon phenomenon. They didn't clearly address some of the real-life contingencies that could easily arise, creating the possibility that an unexpected emergency could create significant turmoil.

When I raised these matters with my father, he would usually say that everything was fine and shuffle away. The shuffle—my father's signature move. I love it. Cute, clunky, and muffled. In this instance, a nonconfrontational way of dealing with something by not dealing with it. He was generally happy for me to handle it, if I so chose. These legal matters were the sort of nuanced, sometimes tedious business details that my father hated to get mired in, regardless of how important they might be. Truth be told, my father has always been far more drawn to the other side of his personality—his love of Hebrew scripture and tradition, and his work as a scholar and rabbi. He is amazing at that. He is not as passionate about running the family business, though as a respectful son he took on that responsibility out of love for his father.

But I knew that this structure had to be modernized, and I was both equipped to tackle the assignment and the only person willing to take it on. I think that was the biggest reason I got the job—the fact that nobody else wanted it (or thought that it was terribly important). It would be intense, detail-oriented, challenging work—which nobody really loves.

Oh, and another thing. I was also the only member of the family who didn't hate dealing with lawyers.

Under the circumstances, reframing our company's governance documents so as to ensure our sound footing for future generations became my project.

The job took almost a year. I spent countless hours with our company lawyers, drafting, redrafting, and debating the contents of legal documents. One by one, the essential clauses fell into place, creating a clear, tightly organized business structure that could withstand any unforeseen economic or family crisis. The revisions we created would also save significant amounts of money that might otherwise go to taxes, legal fees, and other needless expenses. As we worked our way through the process, I tried to explain these benefits to my father, who remained uninterested. That was okay with me. I pressed on.

Finally, the day came when the documents were ready to sign. The key family members with ownership stakes—my paternal grandparents, my dad, and my aunt—gathered with our small team of lawyers for the event at my grandparents' house in Penn Valley, a suburb of Philadelphia. I felt excited and gratified, knowing that we had come to this important moment in Premier's trajectory, a turning point that would solidify the company structure for generations to come. The papers were passed around the dining room table, and pens were circulated for the signing.

Everyone signed and started gathering their things to leave. "Good job," I said to the group. "I'm glad we got this done—plus we just saved a lot of money."

As I spoke, there were smiles and nods around the table. But my father simply turned to me, his face blank, and said, "That's great, Julie. Now go pick out a dress for your grandmother to wear to dinner tonight."

Woah. That sucked. Now, don't get me wrong, I would do absolutely anything for my grandmother. Plus, picking out clothes with her or for her was one of my favorite things—you should have seen her closet! Still, to quote my favorite movie, *My Cousin Vinny* (yes, it's true; all will become clear as you read on), as Mona Lisa Vito said, "Maybe it was a bad time to bring it up." Maybe that was my dad's way of showing that he still didn't care about the legal underpinnings of our business. Maybe it was his way of diminishing me. Maybe he just really wanted Gram to be ready on time. I didn't know exactly what he meant by it. I just knew I felt like shit.

Welcome to the family business.

Let's be honest, being a leader in a family business *can* be one of the most richly rewarding experiences ever. I have opportunities to lead and drive impactful, meaningful action plans and to take our amazing company to even greater heights of competitiveness and sustainability. I can help our people have meaningful careers (and they certainly help me). And I can carry on our family's legacy.

One of those impactful opportunities arose fairly recently. Having become president of Premier (in 2013) and then CEO (in 2016), I had been leading the organization through a big transition on several fronts (a story I'll recount in more detail later in this book). One aspect of that evolution was shaping Premier from a typical this-is-how-we-do-it kind of family company to one that uses sophisticated methodologies and software to track statistics and trends in our industry, analyzes what those trends reveal about shifting customer demands, and uses that information to identify growth opportunities and drive strategy.

Introducing this philosophy and creating systems to implement my vision throughout a conservative, tradition-oriented organization has definitely not been all sunshine and rainbows. Some of our employees were understandably resistant at first. In a few cases, people who couldn't make the necessary shifts in mindset and working habits decided to take other opportunities outside of the company, and throughout the process others had to move on.

But little by little, people began to buy in to the new approach. They felt my passion about the issue, probably because I talked about it and wrote about it constantly. (When I'm locked onto a topic, I get seriously jazzed!) Slowly, the data-driven culture I was trying to create began to emerge, and our people began to share my passion.

In the midst of this transition, one of our most important executives announced his plan to retire. Matt Miller—always known as Lite—was Premier's vice president of sales. And though I'd known for a while that Lite might be departing soon, I wasn't fully prepared to deal with the reality.

I was unprepared for several reasons. I would be losing an indescribably important member of our senior team—someone who had served me as a guide and mentor. And I would be losing someone with thirty years of experience in the dental industry. Everyone (especially me) loved Lite. I realized that, once Lite left, I would, for the first time, be the single most knowledgeable person on our executive team. That might be a normal position for many CEOs, and, yes, I like to think I'm awesome. But I don't need to be the smartest person in the room, and I also like to have a historical and global perspective through which to view the future. The prospect of losing all that Lite had to offer on that front made me uneasy.

I absolutely needed to find an amazing person for the job—not just somebody good.

Over the preceding year, I had been spending about 50 percent of my time screening candidates for the sales job in anticipation of Lite's departure—and frustratingly coming up with bupkes (that's Yiddish for a big, fat nothing).

Now time was growing short. Lite would be retiring in five months. I'd been hoping for at least a six-month transition to his replacement. Factoring in the time to find this amazing person, that now wouldn't be possible. The pressure was suffocating.

I stepped up the search into an even higher gear. I didn't want an old-school, schmoozing and back-slapping "sales guy" like the ones who dominated the industry in past decades. Because I was pushing Premier to be data-driven, I wanted a sales leader who had competency and passion in this area—someone who looked at things analytically and strategically, and would use those insights to drive sales.

Our outside recruiter scoured other companies in the dental industry looking for someone with those traits, but I didn't click with any of the candidates I met. Realizing that we had to broaden our scope, I directed the recruiter to look outside our industry. Specifically, I suggested we look for a candidate who had worked at AmerisourceBergen. ABC, as it's called, is a giant ($213 billion at the time of this writing), widely respected distributor of health-care products. I figured that a candidate with a successful history at ABC would be a great fit with Premier because our two industries have similar distribution and manufacturing structures.

Still, no luck. No candidate with the right combination of characteristics could be found. Days turned into weeks, weeks into months. Lite would soon be gone, leaving a gaping void in our leadership team and in my psyche. My concern morphed into real anxiety. At 2 AM I found myself binge-watching videos of *The Voice UK* on YouTube rather than sleeping.

Finally, one night—this time at two thirty—I decided to stop watching will.i.am and instead turn my anxiety into productive energy.

I clicked into LinkedIn, typed in AmerisourceBergen, and began to scroll through the profiles of company leaders.

One individual jumped out at me. I'm not sure why. I had defined four types of experience I was looking for, and Penny had only one of the four:

Sales leadership: No
Product analysis: No
Customer retention: No
Strategic analysis: Yes

Aside from working at ABC as a strategic analyst, on paper, Penny had nothing else that I was looking for. She had never sold anything in her life, nor had she been responsible for a sales team. But she was an expert at deeply analyzing markets and devising strategies for success. That talent was at the heart of what I wanted for Premier. I was transfixed by Penny's possibilities, which I somehow sensed were far bigger and more important than her lack of sales experience.

At 4:30 AM, I finally fell asleep. At least I had a plan for the next morning: I'd invite Penny to interview for our sales VP job.

The next day, I printed out Penny's profile to show to Lite and Dalton from marketing, who was also helping me to vet candidates. I waited quietly in the conference room as they sat reading her profile. When they were done, Lite looked up and said, simply, "No."

I laughed, and the three of us talked about Penny's profile in some depth. I explained why her analytic skills could be exactly what Premier needed. At the end of the discussion, I asked my colleagues how they'd rate Penny on a ten-point scale. "Five," they both responded. Clearly not a standing O.

I laughed again. "I'm going to speak with her anyway."

Our recruiter arranged a meeting between me and Penny, and everything about her reinforced my instincts. Within five minutes, I knew that she was the person I'd been looking for, and after half an hour, I was ready to post her name on the office door.

But I still wanted the support, or at least the acceptance, of Lite and Dalton. We are a very collaborative team at Premier, and Penny and Dalton would be working closely together. I told Lite and Dalton, "I've spoken with Penny, and I'd like you to see her as well." I offered no further comments or information. Interviews were arranged for the next few days.

Well, well, well ... After meeting Penny, both Lite and Dalton let me know, "You were right. She's exactly the person we need."

I love it when that happens.

Penny joined us soon thereafter, and ever since she has been helping to make Premier a truly data-driven company. Hiring her—in the face of dissent from smart, experienced executives whose opinions I consider really valuable—has been a great decision for Premier.

A few months later, I decided to do something else differently, this time at a meeting of our advisory board. The group, which meets once a quarter to review our activities and plans and offer useful insights and advice, is composed of mostly non-dental-industry business leaders, Premier's chief financial officer, my dad, my aunt, and me. Since the board had been advising me, the organization had evolved greatly both in terms of structure and talent. In order to put faces with names and give the board members a greater understanding of the structure and our capabilities, I invited several of our recent hires to attend the meeting, explain their roles, and let the board members see the quality of people that the new Premier was now attracting—the people who would be driving our company forward.

The presentations went great. I could see that the board members were impressed. The truth was that we'd brought in some really amazing talent.

Once the Premier team members had left the room, we then turned to our usual board business—discussing the state of the company and our plans for the near future. Goodbye, warm and fuzzy; hello, grill team. Despite the magnificent leadership team we'd been assembling, Premier's sales were flat. And because we'd been making a number of necessary, long overdue investments, our cash flow picture was daunting. I was a little nervous about how the advisory board would react. The members are business leaders whose counsel is always thoughtful and valuable, and I was worried they might feel I'd been misguided and making incorrect decisions.

My emotions came to the surface when Thomas, one of the members of the board, started to speak. Thomas had been an executive with his own family's enterprise, so he has a deep understanding of the business and personal dynamics that come with running a family business.

"Premier is your grandfather's company . . ." Thomas began.

Those few words immediately killed me. I've always considered being CEO of Premier an enormous responsibility, and one of the big reasons is the love and admiration I feel for my grandfather Morton. I would never want to do anything to disappoint him.

So now, having tried to justify to the advisory board the kinds of changes I was making, including the big investments, I was shaken to hear one of the members refer to Premier as "your grandfather's company." I knew it was. That's why this moment was so searing. Was I doing the wrong things, making the wrong decisions? Would Grandpa be upset if he could see what I was doing with his sacred Premier? I started to tear up.

While those thoughts consumed me, Thomas finished his sentence. ". . . but you can't run it like he did. You need to run it for today and for tomorrow. *And that's exactly what you're doing.*"

I exhaled, wiped my eyes, said "Thank you," and gave him a hug.

Thomas grinned. "Now go have a drink," he suggested.

I knew then that Thomas was right about what Grandpa would think—and I was so grateful to him for reminding me of it.

And now I hope you are starting to understand why I love our family business. And great news—you can love yours too (maybe even love it more). As you continue to read through my experiences, familiar or parallel situations should become illuminated, allowing you to devise your own solutions, paths, and fun.

Chapter 1

Julie and the No Good, Horrible, Very Bad Day

I didn't start my working career as a family business leader. In fact, for a time I was determined to avoid what might have seemed like the natural or easiest path for me. It was important for me to prove to people around me—my family members as well as people from the business world in general—that I had the talent, the intelligence, the guts, and the work ethic to succeed in any environment, with or without a hand up. Of course, especially in those early years, I also had to prove it all to myself.

So I spent several years learning, listening, and trying my hand at other kinds of work in organizations and industries far removed from the world of my family's business. I attended Emory University in Atlanta, where I studied political science and Judaic language and literature (JLL). Not exactly typical subjects for an aspiring business leader, but I spoke (and speak) pretty good Hebrew, could understand and read texts, so why not JLL? At the time, Emory didn't have many "Judaically knowledgeable" students, so I was a rare commodity. I became a research assistant to one of my JLL teachers. I also had a Hebrew professor who read newspaper articles to us in between stories about her belly dancing prowess.

As for political science, that choice was driven by my interests in politics, going back to when I would watch White House press secretaries give their briefings on TV. My poli sci classes at Emory were really enriching. My favorite professor, Dr. Merle Black, was an expert in Southern politics—brilliant, relaxed, charming, tough, and subtly funny. He'd gotten interested in politics while observing his parents working as election volunteers in both presidential and congressional elections in their community in the South. Dr. Black recalled watching his mother and the other volunteers counting the votes, which basically involved sorting paper ballots into two piles based on the responses. However, every few ballots, if there were too many votes for the "wrong candidate," those ballots would be changed or discarded without a second thought.

Young Merle Black asked his mother, "Isn't that cheating?" He never did get a solid answer to the question.

So, yes, JLL and poli sci may not seem like an obvious combination. But they were topics that fascinated me and gave me a solid understanding of human behavior, the dynamics of power, and the importance of religious faith.

While studying at Emory, I interned in several positions at CNN. How lucky do you have to be to get an internship at CNN?! One of my assignments was to work on the show *Inside Politics*. My job was simply to do anything and everything that was needed. I even carried Wolf Blitzer's computer bag once. This was in 1992, and, as you can imagine, the drama and the excitement was beyond incredible, especially on election night with Bill Clinton, George H. W. Bush, and Ross Perot vying for the presidency.

Control Room A was the place from which all the state-by-state results were communicated in the form of special video tapes known as Winner Cards. These triggered the on-air announcement of each winner. Many hours into the night, amidst the electric yet controlled chaos, my boss called me over and asked me if I knew who Booker T. Washington was. I said yes, thinking of the famous Black educator from my history classes. Then my boss handed me a tape and said "Bring this to him in Control Room A right now."

I started at my boss blankly. I wasn't quite sure how I was going to do that—Booker T. Washington was dead.

Seeing my confusion, my boss yelled, "He's a producer, and this is the Clinton Winner Card. Get it to Booker in Control Room A *now*!"

Aaaah! I sprinted out of there, got the tape to Booker (who, yes, was a producer at CNN), and told him what it was. Hello, life highlight!

So, if you were watching *Inside Politics* on election night in 1992, now you know that I was there.

I then took a job at the American Israel Public Affairs Committee (AIPAC) in Washington, D.C. Best known for its focus on ensuring strong US support for the nation of Israel, AIPAC is sometimes described as one of the most effective lobbying organizations in the U.S.—which is saying a lot in a country where every industry, social cause, and interest group needs a lobbying effort to advocate for it on Capitol Hill. I spent most of my time at AIPAC working on legislation and member voting, which gave me some useful insights into public opinion, how it's shaped, and why it's so important. These are things I think every business leader needs to understand.

As you can see, these years offered me some valuable learning experiences. But those lessons didn't come without pain.

One of my jobs as a legislative assistant was to compile the voting records for members of Congress on legislation of importance to AIPAC's mission. The most critical dissemination point of these records was during AIPAC'S annual meeting in D.C., when tens of thousands of people gather to lobby their congressional representatives. Depending on the voting record of each member, AIPAC could thank them for their support or ask them for their support in the future. So having accurate information about how the representatives had voted on key pieces of legislation was very important.

The job of compiling this data was handled using Excel, the computer spreadsheet program that has now become ubiquitous, but which was less widely familiar back in 1996. Unfortunately, I wasn't very familiar with it, and I fucked it up pretty badly, mixing up several columns so that members of Congress who actually voted Yes were listed as having voted No, and vice versa. I deserved to be fired—and I was.

Most people have gotten fired at some point in their career. It happened to me. But what for most people is just a temporary setback was, for me, the worst thing that had ever happened in my life. (At least, the worst thing up to that time. Thinking about it from a new vantage point in the world of COVID-19, I'm developing a fresh perspective on that . . .)

My reaction to being fired goes back to my personality. I am super-*über*-Type A—career-driven—and I have been since I was six years old. Always wanting to achieve and constantly planning how to get there, through grade school, high school, college, internships, jobs, graduate school, networking, and sleepless nights worrying about every imaginable detail that I might have gotten wrong, and focusing on the *new* details that I had to tackle the next day. My drive defines me, for good or bad.

So imagine someone with this level of obsession making a mistake and getting fired for it. What would this mean to their sense of self-worth? It would absolutely destroy them—just like it did me. I was humiliated, embarrassed, ashamed. It felt like the destruction of everything I valued—including my sense of self.

At the time, I had just started dating Darryl, the man who is now my husband, and I was already very much in love with him. I was terrified of what his reaction would be to my firing. I was sure he would dump me. I even wondered whether I could get away with not telling him. But eventually I made the call.

I planned to be nonchalant and unbothered. Good luck with that. As soon as he picked up, I started to cry, to the point where I couldn't speak. This of course worried and upset him. Once I was able to tell him what had happened, his response shocked me.

He chuckled and said, "That's it? I thought something was really wrong. It's just a job! You'll get another one."

I told you that I loved him before this call. Well, this comment upped his value even further. It allowed me to put the moment into perspective, and cemented for me the fact that he was (and is) the one and only man for me.

I made my peace with getting fired. In the days and weeks that followed, as I reflected on my time at AIPAC, I realized that being so deeply immersed in the political scene and culture of Washington wasn't for me. (I think this is an attitude that lots of Americans have come to share in the tumultuous years since then.) Maybe leaving AIPAC at that time was the right thing for me—maybe it was meant to be, painful as it was.

But one thing that didn't change in the wake of my departure from AIPAC was my attitude toward work. I will always be the extreme Type A woman that I was in my twenties (and that I have been since elementary school), though I've gotten better at handling disasters—and especially at fending them off before they happen. That's an approach to management that has served me well—including today, when I no longer have to stay up at night wondering whether I might get fired tomorrow. Instead, I have the even longer list of worries that come with being the CEO of a generations-old family enterprise.

I also spent some time at RCN, a fledgling cable TV company based in Princeton, New Jersey. It was a start-up business that had been launched with venture capital funding by an entrepreneur named David McCourt. My job was to manage the marketing effort for RCN in the Philadelphia area, which was already dominated by the rival company Comcast. I found that the experience of having been fired from AIPAC had taught me a valuable lesson—namely, the importance of being intensely detail-oriented. I was guided by that new awareness as I orchestrated the work of my marketing team, leading weekly meetings to make sure that nothing fell through the cracks.

From a business perspective, RCN turned out to be a doomed effort—it ultimately went bankrupt in 2004 after suffering total losses of $4 billion. But working there was an important experience for me. RCN was the first truly "capitalist" enterprise I'd ever worked for. It's where I learned how to operate in a corporate environment, the demands of entrepreneurship, and what it means to compete for market share. I loved it all. It's also where I developed a sense of what professionalism means to me—a combination of self-reflection and willingness to self-correct with the Type A work ethic I'd always brought to any task. Working at RCN meant getting used to operating on overdrive at all times, constantly mastering new skills, and learning from every experience, good or bad. It was grueling and demanding. And I loved it.

Most important, RCN is the place where I realized that being my authentic self meant working to be seen as a leader. That's what the rest of my story has been about.

Of course, that's a lesson I fully learned only in retrospect, looking back on those early experiences. That's how life works. Events that seem random at the time turn out to help shape who we are and the big decisions we make later in life. Studying politics and working in media didn't lead directly to my career in the dental industry. But they taught me ways to think about communication and managing in the public spotlight that have served me well as a CEO. As you look back on your own first career steps, you too may find that seemingly unconnected happenings have become stepping stones to success.

I'm sure the experiences you'll read about in these pages will be different from your own. That's okay. The learnings you can take from them can still be relevant and valuable for you. The time will come when you'll face decisions not unlike the ones I've faced as a family business leader. When that happens, knowing what I did may be helpful—not in a rigid "You must do X" kind of way, but as an extra glimpse into the way the life of the leader unfolds.

And also, as a source of encouragement. After all, you'll learn that I screwed up plenty of times—and I'm still going. Why can't you do the same?

Chapter 2

One Hundred Years and Counting

Today, a couple of decades after being fired from AIPAC, I am CEO of Premier Dental Products. It's not a company whose name everybody knows, and it's not an industry that millions of kids dream about joining someday. Dentistry is a big business, of course. But it's not Hollywood, it's not Google, it's not fashion or high tech or pro sports—which means it's not sexy, right?

Wrong! It's dentistry, and to me—and many others—it's just as cool as self-driving cars. Think about it: All of us in the world of dentistry are providing people the tools for better oral health. We are making them look better, feel better, have less pain, and be more self-confident. What's not awesome about that?!

Of course, I'm not a dentist; I don't even play one on TV. So what makes me so interested in dentistry?

The big reason is history. Our company has been a successful business serving dentists and their patients for over a century, started, run, and led for that entire time by one family—my family. That alone is reason enough for me to love the business. To know that a single entrepreneur, my great-grandfather Julius, started a business in 1913 that would sustain four generations, support hundreds of families, and help provide greater health and happiness for millions more—to me, that's fantastic.

So I love Premier for the legacy it represents, I love it for the connections it has created, and I love it because my grandfather loved it. Aside from his wife, my grandfather's greatest love was Premier. He loved the people, the industry, and the opportunities that Premier made available. He understood the dynamics of business, and how to build a great one. I share his passion for Premier and his obsessive desire to continue to make it great.

On many occasions, people who knew my grandfather have told me, "We can see that you love the business the way Morton did, because you deal with it the way he did." I consider that the ultimate compliment.

Selfishly, I also love Premier because it gives me the opportunity to build something great, to shape something meaningful and impactful. It provides me with a space in which I can learn and grow, make mistakes, reach my goals, and earn the respect of others. It allows for me to learn from all of our tremendous people. It gives me a way to serve as an example to my children; to show them the meaning of love, respect, hard work, and opportunity; to teach my daughter independence; and to teach my son the importance of a strong partner.

I love Premier because, in so many ways, it gives me my identity.

More than one hundred years is a long time for a business to be in existence. Premier is older than many of the most well-known and successful companies in America, from Disney to Marriott, State Farm to Motorola, Caterpillar to Boeing.

For a business to be successful, wholly family-owned, and growing over that length of time is truly remarkable. The obvious question—one I've been asked countless times—is: how did it happen?

My answer is: where do I start?

There is a long list of essential things needed for a family enterprise to remain successful for over a century. There are family values and unwritten understandings. There is the desire for continuity and the willingness to pursue it. There is understanding of the market, the industry, and the changing needs of customers. There are legal documents and succession plans. There is the foresight and the wisdom needed to turn the company's daily running and vision over to the professionals. There is the financial philosophy of both the organization and the family. There are counselors, advisors, and mentors whose opinions need to be heard. There is the recognition of fragility, the need for humility, and the appreciation of those who work for our collective success.

And there are 65,734,228 other reasons. Give or take a few.

Thankfully, in 1913, my great-grandfather Julius had the remarkable understanding that health care would always be an essential need. Happily, my grandfather Morton was able to take the company that Julius founded and wisely shepherd it to new heights of achievement.

Two of my grandfather's deepest commitments were to branding and quality. During the time of his leadership, branding as we know it today wasn't really a "thing"; Mr. M. would never have dreamed of hiring a multimillion-dollar consultant to generate brand concepts or logo designs calculated to build brand image equity. But he and the incomparable team at Premier had an instinctive understanding of the importance of the Premier brand, its capabilities, and its reputation.

They also took tremendous pride in the quality of the goods and services they offered. I mean, just look at our name—Premier. Need I say more? Quality is essential in all products, and back in the day when government regulation was much less common and less strictly enforced, it was even more important, especially when it came to oral health and the products that dentists used. It was vital to Premier's brand and reputation that all of our products be stellar and perform above expectations. Understanding this, my grandfather was fanatical—appropriately so—about the branding and quality associated with Premier.

I would say that, in my grandfather's mind, almost as important as branding and quality was sales. By that I don't mean revenues, though of course the necessity of revenues to keep the company going and growing goes without saying. I mean the character of salespeople, how they comported themselves, how they represented Premier, how they defined the products, and how they sold them. He hired people he respected, he treated them fairly, and he insisted that they pass along the same level of respect and integrity to the customers they served. And he would frequently remind everyone who worked for Premier, "Always ask for the order. The worst they can say is no." This Mortonism may seem pretty basic, but it is understatedly brilliant, and strangely it's a piece of fundamental business wisdom that not many people employ.

Like branding, another concept of business leadership that people didn't talk about much back then was "corporate culture," but this too was a topic that my grandfather instinctively understood. Every month, the entire Premier team celebrated what they called Cake Day, marking the birthdays of everyone who'd been born that month. All of those working at our corporate headquarters would gather in the lunchroom where there would be a large cake—sometimes even an ice cream cake—covered with the names of everyone celebrating a birthday that month. Cake Day provided an opportunity to bring everyone together, enhance the sense of camaraderie that united us, and get a brief state-of-the-company report delivered by Mr. M.

My grandfather's speeches were something special, several notches above the usual business boilerplate. He always had something meaningful, wise, and touching to say. They could also be exciting, especially when he was energized about a new product we were launching. For example, he was especially excited about our launch of 2pro®, a disposable prophy angle—one of those dental tools with a soft, rotating cup on the end to apply prophy paste on a patient's teeth. 2pro is special because it operates with pistons instead of gears, and it's translucent so that you can see the gadget's inner workings. Doesn't sound exciting, but trust me, these angles are very cool—which is why my grandfather always referred to them as, "You know, my favorite, those little green things."

Sometimes Mr. M. got a little carried away when he was pumped up about a new product. On one Cake Day, he launched into a speech that captured his passion not just about the latest new product but also about the value of the Premier brand. To emphasize his commitment to quality and the protection of our precious reputation above all else, he closed his remarks by saying, "I can sell anything with the Premier name on it. I can sell a bottle of shit if it says Premier on the label. But I'll only sell it once!"

As a woman in business, I must also explain that I love Premier because it provides me with a connection with some amazing women leaders.

My grandmother, Malvina Charlestein—Mr. M.'s wife—was an absolute force. She was the definition of a matriarch and epitomized the adage, "Behind every strong man is an even stronger woman." Gram was stunning, fearless, determined, and unforgiving. And her strength of will and persuasiveness were exhibited in many forms.

My aunt, Malvina's daughter, whom we all call Dodo, was a huge baseball fan who also married a huge baseball fan. Like the rest of the family, they settled in the Philadelphia area, and they naturally became dedicated fans of the Phillies, the city's major league baseball team.

Then tragedy struck. While still a young man and a father to a two-year-old daughter, my uncle Alan began to show symptoms of nervous degeneration. Eventually he was diagnosed with amyotrophic lateral sclerosis (ALS), the incurable illness better known by the name of its most famous victim—Lou Gehrig. It's a terrible affliction that is terminal in 100 percent of cases.

Gram swung into action. As I said, my aunt and uncle's favorite activity was baseball. Some of my most fun memories are of being allowed to go to their community-league baseball games. So for my grandmother and aunt, baseball was the place to start. Gram tracked down the owner of the Phillies, a man named William Y. Giles. Somehow, in this era before email, Facebook, or LinkedIn, she made a direct connection with the owner and arranged a face-to-face meeting. Remarkably (although not really if you knew Gram), she convinced him to make ALS an official charitable cause of the Philadelphia Phillies. The team partnered with the ALS Association Greater Philadelphia Chapter, headed up by my aunt, to support the effort to find a cure for ALS and to help those victimized by the disease.

To this day, the Phillies continue to hold an annual Phillies

Phestival at the ballpark every June, with the proceeds dedicated to finding a cure for ALS. The club has raised tens of millions of dollars for the cause.

Another cause that my grandmother embraced was that of freedom for Soviet Jews. After the Six-Day War in 1967, the Soviet Union broke off diplomatic relations with Israel, and also began denying exit visas to Soviet Jews who sought to emigrate to Israel. A period of intense discrimination and persecution followed, with Jews denied the rights of cultural freedom and self-expression granted to most other minorities in the USSR. Jews throughout the worldwide diaspora, especially in the United States, began to speak up against this behavior, and my grandmother was one of the leaders of this movement in the Philadelphia area. Along with my parents and cousins, my grandmother lobbied U.S. government officials, from Congress to the White House, to put pressure on the Soviet leaders to grant freedom to their Jewish citizens. One hilarious but effective example was when she helped lead a boycott of the Bolshoi Ballet company when they visited the U.S. To draw attention to the cause, she even marched on a picket line outside the theatre wearing a ballerina's tutu.

These efforts paid off. In 1969, the Soviet Union reluctantly began to allow some Jews to leave for Israel, and in the early 1970s, about 150,000 Jews left Russia for Israel in what came to be called the Aliyah. The departure of these Jews—many of them highly educated professionals—produced a brain drain that contributed to the economic decline and ultimately the collapse of the Soviet Union in 1989.

After that collapse, between 1989 and 2006, another 1.5 million Jews left the former Soviet Union in the so-called Soviet Aliyah. About 60 percent settled in Israel; most of the remainder came to the U.S. It's possible that none of these Jews would have enjoyed the freedom they did without the advocacy work of powerful citizen leaders like my grandmother.

My grandmother's ability to make things happen the way she wanted them to was also clearly demonstrated in our family activities.

Over the years, a number of our clan would participate in extended family vacations, including one year at a dude ranch in Arizona. That was the year when I had gotten engaged to Darryl, and he was invited to join us on our trip west. It was an eye-opening experience for him. The Charlestein family are not low-maintenance people, and at that time, this applied especially to our choice of food. My sister and I were ridiculously fussy—we insisted that our diet contain no oil, no fat, no butter, no cheese. Frankly, we were obnoxious about it.

But Gram understood. Somehow she made our wishes known to the management of the dude ranch and ensured that they were taken seriously. In fact, an entire section of the refrigerator in the kitchen of the main dining hall was set aside specifically for Charlestein family delicacies, from skim milk to specially-prepared low-fat jelly beans. I remember Darryl listening in amazement as I ordered my breakfast from a puzzled young waiter: egg whites prepared with no butter or oil, and a bagel with its bread scooped out and filled with fat-free cream cheese.

On our way home, Darryl commented, "Well, I certainly learned something on this vacation."

"What did you learn?" I asked him. "That the Charlestein family is nuts?"

"No, I learned that the menu is only a suggestion!"

Of course, my grandmother didn't always get her way. One of

her projects was the creation of a pre-digital matchmaking service to pair up some of the eligible young Jewish singles she met in the Philadelphia area. Gram created detailed handwritten lists of the young men and women she wanted to link up, filled with details about their backgrounds and interests. Her secret mission in all this was to find a husband for my aunt Ellyn. The rest of the family realized this when we noticed that all of the most attractive men on Gram's list seemed to get Ellyn as their "perfect match."

This became fodder for a hilarious song that we performed at Gram's seventy-fifth birthday party. Our song told the story of her matchmaking service, and each verse ended with the same repeated lyric: "Lucky you—your date is Ellyn!"

Despite Gram's best efforts, Ellyn ended up marrying someone wonderful whom she found on her own.

All in all, although my grandmother never held a traditional leadership position, she was a person of power. I am blessed to have both, and I give a lot of the credit to my good fortune in being Malvina Charlestein's granddaughter. For this reason, when people ask me how I feel about being a woman leader in business, I usually respond that, for me, it's a nonissue.

And because Premier is a family business, the company culture is a blend of corporate influences—the challenges of the dental industry, for example—and personal traits and values that capture what it means to be a Charlestein.

As I've explained, I started my career in the realm of media and politics, with no intention of becoming part of the family business. But since joining Premier and rising to the role of CEO—not an easy process, as you'll hear—I've come to learn all there is to know about Premier and its role in the health-care industry, especially the world of dentistry. I've discovered that, although we are in the top tier of

developers and manufacturers of dental products, we are *not* in the
top five when measured by revenues or profits. To me, this is one of
the most amazing things about Premier. Even though our competitors
are multibillion-dollar companies with tens of thousands of dollars
to my one, we can "hang" with them. We compete strongly in the
marketplace, with many of our products leading in their categories,
all thanks to Premier's people, their fortitude, their creativity, and the
evolutionary capabilities they've shown in an ever-changing business.

As a result, I don't operate like a relatively small player among
giant competitors. Instead, I go into every meeting—whether with
customers, suppliers, or financiers—behaving like the CEO of a
major player . . . because that's what I am. Premier is a business that
is impactful and important, and I conduct myself in accordance
with that truth. I serve on many boards of advisors with my counterparts from larger companies, and I never feel out of place. (Well,
occasionally, when I'm sitting at a conference table surrounded by
people with PhDs, I'll admit to feeling a bit intimidated.)

It just goes to show that perception and reality are two very
different things, both very important. In the world of dentistry,
Premier is perceived to be much larger than we are, due to our
standing in the industry, our legacy, and our continued successes.

Once, I was having dinner with a long-time friend and industry colleague, chatting about some of the things that Premier was
working on. He chuckled and said, "You definitely punch above
your weight!" For a moment, I didn't know what he meant—I even
wondered whether I should feel insulted. But then I realized that
being called skinny is a good thing. Hello, Joan Rivers—you can
never be too rich or too thin!

The wonderful Premier legacy that my grandfather helped to
build has led to some memorable moments in our history.

In 2008, for my grandfather's ninetieth birthday, we held a huge industry celebration. The American Dental Association happened to be having their annual meeting in Philadelphia, our corporate base, which provided the perfect opportunity to highlight Premier. So we had a blowout event at the National Constitution Center. We even had a "Declaration of Morton" drafted as a piece of art that we had everyone sign in "Signers' Hall"—a super cool experience. Although at the time I was just a mid-level manager at Premier, as a family member I was asked to serve as the emcee for the event. In addition to being a joyous a celebration for my grandfather, it also served as a coming-out party for me as the future leader of Premier.

Practically everyone from the industry was there. I found out later that the relatively few people who hadn't been invited—including some of our competitors—were actually pissed. Love that! The other amazing thing about the night was that all of the giants of the industry—the CEOs of all of our major customers, academics, leading researchers—all gave speeches in recognition of my grandfather, his accomplishments, his business acumen, and, most important, his truly rare, special, and beloved personality.

In planning the event, we decided that we wanted to have our guests leave with a gift representative of the celebration. We wondered what to do in honor of a 90-year-old dental-industry icon. Finally, we decided on a simple frame, etched with the event's name and date, and containing a card that read:

"Remember who you are" —*Morton Charlestein*

To this day, I see this frame on display in the offices of many of our industry partners.

I never miss an opportunity to draw connecting lines between Premier's amazing legacy and the business I am now proud to run—for example, at trade shows.

I attended one recently that was hosted by one of our major customers, a dental distribution business. At that trade show, each developer/manufacturer like Premier had a booth. The host company's sales representatives would rotate through these booths learning about the various products and technologies. Each opportunity to speak to a group of reps lasted a maximum of five minutes.

The show was officially opened, and the first group of attendees came through on their rotation. I very excitedly chatted with them about Premier, our products, and how our teams could best work together. They thanked me, and as they were meandering away to make room for the next group, one of the reps pulled me aside. "You should really come and work for us," he said.

It was obvious that he had no idea that Premier was a family business, or that I was the CEO drawn from the fourth generation of its family owners. So I just smiled, thanked him for the compliment, and told him "I love Premier."

He was insistent. "This could be a great opportunity for you. You could do great things. I have never seen someone so energetic, so passionate, and so knowledgeable."

"Thanks anyway," I said, "But I'm still sticking where I am."

A similar moment with a different spin happened at a recent meeting with executives from a financial group. The tone of the conversation was testy; the bankers were challenging me on many fronts, questioning my experience, my knowledge, and my strategic insights. This didn't bother me. I knew what I was talking about, and I knew that I knew.

Then, as if trying to deliver the ultimate insult, one of the bankers declared, "The fact is that we don't even know anything about you. We don't even know anything about Premier."

My response was genuinely enthusiastic. "Great! Let's talk about it. Premier is my absolute favorite subject!"

This completely disarmed them.

But that comes naturally to me. I am forever Premier's greatest champion, brand ambassador, and salesperson. As Grandpa used to say, "Remember who you are"—and I do, every day.

QUOTE UNQUOTE

"Remember who you are."

When I was a small child, I took this favorite Mortonism literally: I figured my grandfather wanted me to memorize my name, address, and telephone number. Good advice for a six-year-old!

But as I grew up, I learned about its deeper meanings. Among other things, it means to be mindful of all you've inherited from those who came before you—not in terms of wealth, but character. It's a call to use these inheritances to shape who you are and to help you become a solid representative of what they stand for.

"Remember who you are" is also a reminder of the importance of authenticity—revealing and reflecting your genuine self rather than trying to play a role in an effort to impress other people. As a CEO, I've discovered that simple honesty and transparency are two of the most powerful tools I can use to make strong, lasting connections. Thank you to my grandfather for teaching me this lesson.

Chapter 3

The Boss Is the Boss

How, when, and why you decide to join a family business can have a huge impact on your subsequent success.

I'd been working at RCN for about a year when my father started calling me to talk about my career. At first, the questions were open-ended—things like, "How's everything going with your job?" But soon, he began to ask me directly whether I would consider joining Premier.

For a while, I held back. I didn't say a flat-out no, but I didn't say yes. I wanted to learn a bit more before making such an important decision. So I asked my father, "What would that look like?" and we talked a little about how I would probably start in a mid-level managerial position, which would give me the opportunity to learn the business without having to shoulder a lot of responsibility initially.

I also wanted some outside perspectives on what it would mean to become part of Premier. I spoke to a family business consultant, as well as with some trusted friends who worked in family businesses and in the dental industry. The more I learned and thought about it, the more I felt that I could probably do well and grow within Premier. I just didn't realize how difficult it would be, both from a purely business standpoint and from a familial one.

As a stepping stone toward making a firm decision about Premier, I agreed to take a part-time job there. I figured it would be a good way to get a feeling for the company

As I thought about making a final decision on whether I wanted to build a career at Premier, I decided it might be wise to attend business school and learn more about the skills required to succeed as a company leader.

I brought this idea to my father. His response was, "I think graduate school is a great idea. Why not go for art history, or something that really interests you?"

It was a surprising answer, but it reflected one great thing about my father and our family business: there were no expectations and certainly no pressure on me or my siblings to make our futures at Premier. I appreciated that.

However, when my dad suggested art history, I actually laughed at his response. I told him that I was happy to hear his willingness to enrich my personal education and support my interests, but if he ultimately wanted me to help him run Premier, I should probably focus on business school. We agreed that I would take one class and see what I thought. I did, I loved it, and I enrolled at Temple University.

I know this is not the most typical story of a business school student. I have many friends who always knew they wanted to go into business and who worked very hard to get into top programs. Many of these same people also sought out specific jobs, connections, and internships along the way. I wasn't that thoughtful—in my case, the path was more circuitous and improvised, although I landed in the right place in the end.

Maybe there's a valuable lesson in this. If you're one of those people with a clear sense of direction from your childhood, that's great. Whatever your goal is, pursue it. But if, like me, you're uncertain as to what you want to do—but not who you want to be—don't worry. In my experience, it worked to try different things, explore options, and not be afraid to experiment. It may take you a little longer to figure out where you belong, but so what?

I ended up feeling very glad that I went to business school for two main reasons: optics and credibility. Clearly, if I went to work at Premier, it would be obvious to all that I had gotten the job as a result of nepotism—an unavoidable, unassailable fact. So how would I combat—or at least soften—the perception that I might not be qualified for the job? Going to business school showed my willingness to commit. Of course, working outside of Premier, as I'd done for several years, helped to demonstrate these qualities as well, probably even more than the business degree I earned. But in combination, they made the case for the validity of my position.

If you're wondering about the value of the classes I took in business school, I wouldn't say that they taught me the nuts and bolts of running a business. This isn't surprising—how much of your high school or college calculus are you putting into use in the real world? However, I did learn to think in a more holistic way, looking at the totality of a business situation as opposed to considering only one specific outcome or issue.

I also learned the importance of collaboration and listening—two things that may sound basic and obvious, but that were eye-opening for me as a young twenty-something without that mindset.

Of course, being in an academic environment is always enriching, and having the ability to learn for the sake of learning is an incredible luxury. I would say that was the case for all of my classes, with the exception of statistics—I so sucked at that class!

To sum up, while I enrolled at Temple essentially to establish my legitimacy and, of course, to improve my business skills, I came out with a greater sense of confidence and a broader perspective on things—two qualities that have served me well in business and life.

Eventually, the intriguing possibilities of the family business—and my father's continued entreaties to join him there—convinced me to become part of Premier. I soon discovered that being a G4 (fourth-generation) family business member can be a struggle.

I joined Premier in 2001 as a product manager, responsible for our ultrasonic insert line. I had to oversee the development, launch, sales, and marketing of those products.

Maybe to a family business outsider, it sounds like a sweet deal—joining a company where your father is the CEO and everyone knows you're a member of the founding family. And, in some ways, it is. But I was working for a father who, while loving and encouraging, definitely challenged many of my decisions. Not through obvious gestures—my father's personal style is totally non-confrontational. Instead, he used small, symbolic acts to make sure I knew my role.

Some of his tactics were very subtle. For example, there was the time I was away from the office on maternity leave.

The fact that I was expecting a baby is a story unto itself. From a very young age, I had determined that I would be independent, successful, and have a strong career. In my thinking, that meant to be a constant driver. Always pushing, working, trying to achieve, trying to accomplish, and trying to learn.

I wasn't sure that children were a part of that picture. I spent much of my first pregnancy coping with anxiety about what my life would become. How would I continue pursuing my life's goals? What did I have to do to make sure that those would not be overshadowed by the new responsibilities I was taking on as a parent?

I anticipated that combining motherhood with career success at a high level would not be easy. I definitely wasn't wrong about that. I was not what I think of as a typical mother—someone for whom parenthood was a lifelong goal. In fact, I was deeply unsure about having children. I had never had that need, desire, or longing as so many women speak about. When I saw babies, it didn't move me in any way. (To tell the truth, I still don't really like to be with babies. Even my nieces and nephews, cute as they are, don't give me a thrill.) My mind was centrally and obsessively focused on my career; my deepest longing was for success and independence. And deep down, I didn't believe that could be congruent with motherhood.

Add to all this the fact that I am intensely body-conscious and fundamentally pretty selfish—you can see that I am not necessarily someone who has the makings of an ideal mother.

As a result, having children was something that I didn't really think much about. But I *did* know that, if I were to have children—if—it wouldn't be until well into my marriage. First, I wanted to travel, and work, and have time for us. I knew that if we had kids, life would never be the same, and it certainly wouldn't be all about me. (Like I said, selfish.) So I made sure that my husband and I were clear on this. Before we got married, I told him it would be at least five years before kids would be part of the picture.

That five-year mark came, and there actually wasn't a huge conversation between Darryl and me about parenthood. It was basically like, "Okay, we're at five years. What do you think?"

I was really fine either way, leaning more toward not. However, my husband *did* want kids. So since at that point I didn't feel that strongly about it, I decided to go ahead.

As it turned out, this was a fantastic decision. We now have two fabulous children who enrich me and the world every day.

But as you can see, it wasn't an easy or automatic choice for me. So when I became pregnant for the first time, I was terrified about what becoming a mother might mean. I hated the idea of losing the freedom and independence that I'd gotten from being a professional and having my own income to rely upon. And I was afraid that becoming a mother would change me. (Hello! Of course it would!)

So I kept working through my maternity leave, absolutely determined to hang on tight to the activities that for me symbolized freedom, power, and control.

One day, I was on the phone having a conference call with Premier's top executives. Toward the end of the call, my father casually announced that I would now be overseeing all of the product managers—a substantial increase in responsibility.

WHAT?! Of course, I was excited to have my capabilities recognized. But I was also shocked. My father and I had never discussed this possible promotion or planned for it in any way. The way he made the announcement was reflective of his indirect style, and sent me into super-crazed-anxiety mode as to how I would succeed in this new role while also being a new mother.

In this way, it was a typical reflection of my relationship with my father—a strange blend of love, challenge, and respect.

Sometimes, my father's approach to business, though always wrapped in caring, put me in a position that was awkward and frustrating. I once had the opportunity to negotiate what would have been a very important distribution agreement for the Chinese market. A big deal, right? Premier already had a presence in that country, but it was lackluster at best. When a partner approached us about working with them to open up China, I could see it was an important strategic move.

My father, however, opposed it out of a sense of loyalty to our existing partner in the country, and would not let me move forward with the opportunity. He was the CEO then; it was his right to make the decision, and I respected that. Even though I knew I was correct, my father was unwilling to change his view due to allegiance and emotion. It's not necessarily the best approach to leadership, although maintaining certain relationships is important. It's frustrating, but probably easier to accept when the boss isn't your father. Just another day at the office—an example of the kind of experience that was built into having my father as my business superior. The boss is the boss, and he was the boss.

I was learning how complicated it can be to navigate the intersection between business and family values. I know my father intimately—his motivations, his personality. He deeply values qualities like modesty, inclusion, and being a good teacher. I honor these values, yet I'm also very focused on independence, drive, and success. When you're a business leader with an intimate knowledge of your "business partner"—in this case, my father—it puts you at both an advantage and a disadvantage. Like any child, you want and need to differentiate yourself from your parents. But as a company leader, you also need to sustain and inculcate their values; they are important, and they allow for a smooth working relationship. In the world of family business, the drive for change and progress needs to be coupled with emotional analysis, humility, and patience. This is where the "family" in family business comes in, making the role of the company leader different than elsewhere.

The ultimate disappointment for me in the early years of working at Premier came in the form of a supposed promotion. After I'd been at the company for a while, my father told me that, when the current president of Premier retired, he wanted me to step into that position. I was excited and felt proud that my father would consider me for that role—until he added, "Of course, this will be a titular role."

In other words, I would be president in name only. All the decisions would continue to be made by my father, the CEO. My excitement turned into confusion and anger.

I turned down the offer. I would wait until I could be the real president.

Years later, when I did agree to become president, a similar dynamic played out. This time, I did take on the president's role, while my father kept his title as CEO. It took me a little while to understand the implications of this arrangement. I soon realized that, as president, I was not all-powerful; although I had significant control over daily operations, the CEO retained the right to overrule me and to establish policies that I might or might not agree with. This was extremely difficult and obstructive for me. But again, the boss is the boss, and he was the boss. I needed to accept that. Hard to do. I felt trapped and became very depressed. I questioned whether or not I should leave, if I could leave, and all of the ramifications if I did.

During this period, I actually looked closely at some other business opportunities, including a potential partnership with a powerful individual outside of Premier. This was an intriguing and tempting possibility. However, I ultimately decided not to pursue it. I'd become interested in a long-term career at Premier, and I'd found I was willing to work within the limitations of my role as president—at least in the short term, while waiting for the possibility to expand into the dual role of president and CEO.

But the fact that I had other options outside of Premier made a big difference in my mindset. I felt validated by the interest shown in me by other organizations. Somewhat paradoxically, it was only once I decided that I actually could leave, and that I knew that I could be successful on my own, that I could move forward within Premier.

Making this hard but essential decision reflected one of the first and most important lessons I learned about the special pitfalls of family businesses. The relationship between my father and me was heavily laden with the kinds of psychological and emotional complications that many parents and children share. That's natural. But once I stepped into the new role of being my father's employee and one of the company leaders helping to shape the business for years to come, I had to figure out how to put that baggage aside—how to respond to his behavior just as I would if I were working for any company, with a boss who hadn't raised me.

That wasn't easy to do—in fact, sometimes I'm still working on it. But understanding the real nature of the challenge I face makes all the difference.

QUOTE UNQUOTE

"Sorry—I'm not you, and you're not him." My father lived his life with ultimate respect for his father. Revering him, and serving him with deference. I can understand that reverence: My grandfather was a tremendous man—wise,

humble, gentle yet tenacious, philanthropic, and joyful . . . a man to be admired. But when my father and I, over the years, had conversations about my role in the family business, he was often surprised by what he perceived to be my lack of appreciation—the reason being that I did not treat him with same adulation he extended to my grandfather.

My father often said to me, in amazement, "I never had conversations like these with my father."

My reply was always the same: "Sorry—I'm not you, and you're not him."

Chapter 4

Pillows and Pajamas

Adventures of a Type A Working Mom

The late 1990s and the early 2000s were a time when I was under a lot of pressure to learn as much as I could as fast as I could. I'd earned my graduate degree (a master's in business with a concentration in marketing) in 2000, I'd joined Premier as a product manager in 2001, and I was mastering both the peculiarities of the dental industry and the challenges of working in a family business with my father as my boss. That would have been more than enough to keep me busy. But I also had a lot to learn on the home front, because, as I've mentioned, these were the years when I was launching my family.

Yes, I'd always known (and worried) that becoming a mother would transform my life. But until I became pregnant, I didn't really get the reality of how much I would have to learn. This was by choice. I never read any books on pregnancy and parenthood. Darryl and I also made the conscious decision not to listen to the well-meaning advice offered by practically everyone we knew based on little more than their personal experience as parents. "Millions of people do this, right?" I said to myself. "How hard can it be? I'll figure it out."

I did figure it out—but it wasn't always easy.

For months after your baby is born, you have frequent pediatrician appointments. The baby is weighed and measured, shots are administered, and questions about sleeping, crying, feeding, and so on get answered. This was good, because our pediatrician was the one person that Darryl and I were willing to learn from when it came to our little Ruby. So I decided I would turn to her whenever we had a problem.

This decision kicked in one day when it suddenly became clear to me that I had absolutely no idea what I was doing. In fact, I was a basket case. So I made an appointment with Dr. Rosenblum.

When the three of us—mommy, daddy, and baby—arrived at the doctor's office, she was surprised to see us, since we had just been there a few days ago. "What's wrong?" she asked. "Does she have a fever, is she sleeping okay?"

I responded, "I don't know what I'm doing."

"Don't know what you're doing with what?" the doctor asked.

I pointed to Ruby, sitting there in her detachable car seat. "With this. I don't know what I'm doing with this."

"And you made an appointment for *that*?" the doctor asked.

She went on to tell Darryl and me that we were good, caring, smart, and loving parents, and that, while we would make mistakes, we would not do anything to hurt Ruby.

"Thanks," I said, "But I still don't know what to do. Like what do I do at 10 AM and then at 2 PM?"

"Goodbye," Dr. Rosenblum said with a smile as she kicked us out of her office.

I also discovered that, when you're a parent, many of the things that you simply have to know are local "secrets" that are not written down anywhere—things like the best place to buy a stroller. Which parks are the baby-friendly places for walks. Where you can sit outside and have frozen yogurt. Where to feed the ducks. Which nail place will do your kid's nails for two dollars. Which activities to enroll your toddler in. What preschool to send your child to. Before I was pregnant with Ruby, I didn't know or care about any of these things—and in fact I didn't even know that I didn't know about them. Suddenly I had to master a whole new set of skills and information that was just as important and complicated as reading a spreadsheet or managing a departmental budget.

As I've mentioned, I am a Type A woman—driven, impatient, goal-oriented. I decided I should apply this approach to parenthood and set about planning Ruby's perfect babyhood.

I learned that, in the Philadelphia suburbs where my husband and I lived, there are two must-dos for young parents and their offspring: Magic Moments and Sally's Music Circle. Getting into these programs was the equivalent of earning early admission to MIT—or "the gateway to Harvard," as many mothers call it—which meant I would settle for nothing less for Ruby.

Magic Moments was a weekday program for two-year-olds taught by Ina. She was—and is!—everything you could want in a toddler teacher: engaged, fun, cool, and never takes herself too seriously. Ina's class was a big draw for the local mothers. From speaking to other mothers who were in the know, I learned that the key was getting into the Friday class. Two reasons. Number 1: The Friday class incorporated songs and activities for the Jewish Sabbath, so it was more festive and more interactive than the other days. Number 2: Fridays are when most working mothers take the class, which allows for a few hours of special bonding time with their kids. These two elements make Friday Magic Moments the hottest ticket. So as soon as your kid turns six months old, if you have any hope of getting into Friday's Magic Moments, it's your duty to start with the calls, the paperwork, and the registration forms.

Thankfully, I was able to get Ruby enrolled in the Friday Magic Moments class. And four years later, her brother Maccabi followed in her footsteps.

As I write these words, Ruby is on her way to an Ivy League college, and Maccabi is a sushi chef apprentice and taking all honors high school classes. Clearly the work of Ina! And of Ruby and Maccabi's determined Type A mother (as well as their supportive dad).

Another of the millions of things that I hadn't realized I needed to develop was a repertoire of children's songs. That's where Sally's Music Circle came in. It's a weekly music program led by Sally, who has a PhD in music, for mothers and their infants. Everyone sits in a circle and learns songs and plays baby-style "instruments"—not violins, oboes, or timpani but rhythm sticks, bells, and, for those who are really ambitious, the triangle.

Sally's was even more difficult to get into than Magic Moments. You need to sign up for Sally's when you're pregnant. Kids are eligible to participate when they are three months old. Since I was due to give birth in June, a September start was what I needed. That's a very desirable date, because it coordinates with the regular school year. So as soon as I leaned about Sally's, I got us enrolled. Thanks to my hours at Sally's, I am a virtuoso on the egg shaker—something like a maraca, but shaped and sized for baby hands. (Hey, it's not as easy as it looks!)

However, before Ruby reached the three-month mark, I didn't have the benefit of Sally's music knowledge. I hadn't yet learned

"John the Rabbit," "Five Little Ladybugs," "The Wheels on the Bus," or even "If You're Happy and You Know It." So when I brought Ruby home from the hospital, I was at a loss at those moments when nothing will make a baby happy except a song. What was I supposed to do when she cried? How was I supposed to calm her down when she was upset? What was I supposed to do to keep myself amused while bouncing her on my lap or patting her on the back to make her burp? Saying "Shush, shush" over and over again will only get you so far.

For some mysterious reason, Will Smith came to mind. One day, when the usual shushing and bouncing wasn't working, I started singing the theme song from *The Fresh Prince of Bel-Air.* It worked—no crying!

That song got me through those tough first months of motherhood until Sally's could kick in. If you and I ever meet, ask me to sing it for you—I've got it down. I am from Philadelphia, after all.

Being a Type A woman, my instinct is to plan my life and work down to the last detail. Unfortunately, as we all know, life has a way of screwing this up.

In 2004, three years after joining Premier as a product manager and two years into my life as a working mom, I was pursuing my career at 150 percent of capacity. One Thursday, I'd just returned home from Las Vegas, where I'd attended Premier's national sales meeting, with Ruby and her babysitter in tow. (I still always try to travel with family when possible, even now that my kids are much older. Family time is still a high priority for us.) On Sunday night, I was scheduled to hit the road again, this time to attend the world's largest international dental meeting in Germany.

In other words, I was living a crazy schedule. And did I mention that I was twenty-four weeks pregnant with my second child?

Absolutely exhausted and feeling not quite right, I decided to check with the doctor before going overseas. My regular OB-GYN was away, creating an added bit of stress for me. The doctor who was covering for him examined me, told me that everything looked okay, and added, "But come in to the hospital over the weekend if you don't feel better."

By Sunday morning, still feeling out of sorts, I decided to go to the hospital, despite suspecting that I was being a hypochondriac and wasting everyone's time. In fact, I was so convinced that "it's probably really nothing" that I went to the hospital by myself, while my husband continued to enjoy his Sunday.

After examining me the doctor announced, "Call your husband and tell him to bring pillows and pajamas, because you aren't going anywhere for a long time."

What?!

So began the longest twelve weeks of my life. Apparently I was in premature labor. I found myself surrounded by an endless stream of doctors, each one offering a more terrifying prognosis than the one before, shooting me up with steroids before I could even ask what was in the syringe. I spent my first two weeks in the hospital catheterized and unable to leave the bed. Then I was told to lie on my left side for twenty-three hours a day (to get as much blood flow to the baby as possible); my only break was for a daily shower. My big outing was getting wheeled upstairs for my weekly ultrasound. This was so exciting I made the attendants wait while I put on my make-up!

Amidst all of this, I of course was also very worried about Ruby. How was she handling my not being around? I did everything I could to make these weeks less stressful for her, including having our babysitter bring Ruby to visit me in the hospital after preschool every day. We played games, she read books about Dora the Explorer, she worked the buttons on my bed. Amazingly, we actually ended up enjoying a lot of fun quality time together. And when I called her preschool teachers to see how she was doing in the midst of this craziness, they said they couldn't believe how unaffected she seemed: "She's as happy and engaging as ever!"

My healthy son Maccabi was born in my 36th week in a trouble-free delivery.

This may seem counterintuitive, but throughout this unbelievably tormenting ordeal, one thing that I kept thinking was, "Thank God I am a working mother." I had a routine and a support system in place that made my life in and out of the hospital work smoothly. It allowed my husband's and my daughter's lives to remain normal, without having to worry about planning, or schedules, or meals, or cleaning. And although I started my career with doubts as to whether motherhood would fit, I'm now eternally grateful to have both.

The moral of the story: *Women should never be afraid to work—but don't overdo it.* Being a mother is never easy; neither is helping to run a company. Combining the two elevates the crazy to new and amazing heights. But with every passing week, you'll find yourself getting stronger and smarter about meeting both challenges. This principle applies to women in every kind of company—including a family business.

Chapter 5

Cheese and Envelopes

Being a G4 family business member with a master's degree in business doesn't insulate you from the kinds of embarrassing rookie mistakes and stressful office conflicts that any other manager may face. After joining Premier, I quickly realized that I had to learn some of the basics of the industry the hard way: by making mistakes and plowing through.

None of these universal challenges were eliminated by the fact that my great-grandfather had founded the business. In some ways, that fact just intensified them.

Don't misunderstand—I am of course grateful for the role that nepotism has played in my life. As a recipient of it, I recognize the blessings it has bestowed on me as well as the expectations that come with it—both positive and negative. When I joined Premier, there were people around me who knew my background and therefore assumed that I would rise to the challenge of becoming an effective business leader. And there were others who assumed that I was an entitled person who planned to skate by without working hard or mastering any necessary skills—which would mean that I would ultimately fail. Some of the people who made that negative assumption, I'm sure, *hoped* I would fail. After all, don't we all enjoy seeing someone who has been given unearned, undeserved privileges fall flat on their face?

I was very aware of all this baggage from the moment I walked in the door. I couldn't change who I was. But I could change the way people perceived me through the way I behaved. I became obsessed with earning my own reputation by building a track record of personal achievements that no one could deny.

So I worked hard, and I worked a lot—a mode of behavior that was not typical of the culture of Premier. For example, when I came in to the office on weekends to take advantage of the time with quiet phones for thinking and planning, I quickly realized that practically no one else was doing the same. Our corporate culture back then was largely one where people were content doing their jobs. Premier was and is a fantastic place to be. There was absolutely nothing wrong with this approach. For me, though, it was confusing. There just wasn't the sense of tension or discomfort that I found important for making the business better, bigger, more profitable, more successful.

Even business activities that seemed basic to me, like preparing in advance for an important meeting, weren't stressed. Maybe it was me. Maybe I was just too highly strung. Probably a bit of both. During my first year at Premier, we had a meeting scheduled with our largest distribution partner—my first meeting with them. I called up our team leader in advance to learn what was planned for the meeting and how I could contribute to it effectively.

"Well, you know, we visit with these folks all the time," he told me. "We know them and they know us. So we really don't need to do anything to prepare."

I thought to myself, *Are you fucking kidding me!* Aloud, I said, "I still think it would be a good idea to put something together."

We gathered our team for a planning session. We reviewed our ongoing business initiatives and upcoming product launches. We talked about how our partner could participate in our efforts and drive sales for the benefit of both companies. We even mocked up some marketing materials to support our messaging.

When the day of the meeting arrived, I was feeling nervous and intimidated. There were just two of us from Premier in the room, while six members of our partner's team were in attendance. One of their category managers terrified me—she would barely even look in my direction, and made no effort to hide her disdain for me.

I got through the meeting with the help of the amazing and laid-back personality of my manager, and we laid a good foundation for promoting the new line of products that I was responsible for. Rather than just cranking out the usual sales based on rote behavior and past expectations, we would use creative thinking and strategic insights to uncover opportunities to build new achievements together.

Today—eighteen years later—most of the people in that room are still in the dental business, and they continue to be close allies and supporters of Premier. When we get together at sales meetings, conferences, or conventions, we sometimes joke about that initial meeting, when I was so nervous and so uncertain as to whether I really belonged in the room. Today, thankfully, those doubts are things of the past, and these business partners have become my friends.

Unfortunately, making my way in an unfamiliar business environment didn't end there.

Like everyone in business, I was very aware of the importance of networking and proud of my ability to engage in it. But in my early days at Premier, I had no way to know the mores, customs, and protocol of the dental industry network. I paid a price for my naïveté during a major dental trade show when I arranged a lunch meeting with a high-ranking executive at a Fortune 500 company—a major customer of ours.

At the appointed time, I greeted the executive near our booth on the trade show floor, and then I innocently took him to eat at the nearby exhibitors' lounge. This made sense to me. After all, I figured, the exhibitors lounge served food, and it wouldn't take us away from the show for too long—so why not?

Unfortunately, the food in the exhibitors' lounge mirrored what you probably ate on deli day at your high school cafeteria, only not as gourmet.

My lunch partner didn't complain, and I thought we had a great meeting. But when I invited him to lunch again several months later, he said, "Okay, but this time, can we *not* go somewhere that serves sweaty cheese?"

Sweaty cheese?! I thought back to our lunch in the exhibitors' lounge, and I suddenly realized what an idiot I'd been! I couldn't believe that I'd taken this executive to the exhibitors' lounge—a realization made all the more excruciating by the fact that he remembered it in such embarrassing and vivid detail!

That's how I learned that the expected thing for a lunch meeting of that kind would be to take your guest to a trendy new restaurant, preferably arriving in a car—maybe even one with a hired driver. Which is what I always do now, of course!

Lucky for me, that executive had—and has—a good sense of humor. He and I are close friends to this day.

During my early years at Premier, there were some people at the company—not many, but some—who were no fans of mine. I'm not sure whether this was driven by my youth, my gender, my family position—or a combination of all three. Either way, not cool. It didn't take long for me to begin noticing little things these people would do and say that were intended to make me stumble and fall . . . as if my own unforced errors weren't enough.

One of these people was an executive at Premier who seemed to resent me and saw me as having a sense of entitlement. This executive was particularly determined to trip me up and embarrass me. No ploy or accusation was too petty or implausible for him. One time, he even demanded to see the envelopes I'd used to mail notes to some of our clients. The reason? He said that he wanted to make sure that the return address was Premier's, and that I wasn't sneaking personal mail through the company! Insane, right?

Luckily, I quickly recognized this animosity, which put me on my guard whenever this executive and I crossed paths.

One day, this same executive—I'll call him Mr. Envelope—passed along a voicemail message to me. It was from a director at a *huge* global consumer products company, wanting to discuss a possible licensing deal involving a trademark Premier owned. Mr. Envelope added his own brief message: "Maybe this is something you can take care of."

My first thought was to wonder why Mr. Envelope hadn't responded to the call himself. After all, it opened up a potentially significant business opportunity for Premier. It wouldn't be an easy deal to arrange, and negotiating the details of such a deal with a high-powered consumer products company would likely be complicated and time-consuming. But if we could pull it off, it would be quite a victory for Premier. Why wouldn't Mr. Envelope be eager to take that call?

But the more I thought about it, the more I realized what his motivation was. Mr. Envelope recognized the complexities of the proposed deal. He understood that there was a good chance the negotiations would come to nothing. And he assumed that, for someone like me—a relative industry novice and not even a company executive—the challenge of negotiating this deal was beyond my capabilities. Mr. Envelope had passed the message along to me in hopes of seeing me fail—and hopefully failing in the most public and embarrassing way possible.

Challenge accepted!

I returned the call. Thus began a lengthy process of exploring what both companies would want and need to make a licensing partnership viable. It took about a month of phone calls, meetings, and discussions. But in the end, the consumer products director and I reached an agreement that left Premier several hundred thousand dollars richer.

Of course, it also left Mr. Envelope feeling like an idiot . . . and me with the personal satisfaction of having shown him very clearly that I wouldn't be fucked with.

It would be nice to think that being part of a family business would protect you from the most vicious forms of office politics. Sometimes, however, others will resent that you're in the family. It's something that I can actually understand, and I've learned to deal with it. People are people—which means a family business isn't devoid of conflict. The conflict may take many different forms, but it never completely disappears.

QUOTE UNQUOTE

"If you quit, then you will be a quitter." —Kimora Lee Simmons, *Life in the Fab Lane*

Ms. Simmons (now Ms. Leissner) is a model, has started several successful businesses, and was married to business mogul Russell Simmons. Clearly Ms. Leissner and I do not have much in common. Yet while watching her reality show, I felt connected to her. Here was a businesswoman raising young children while managing a household and a staff. I could empathize with her struggles, and I found it cathartic, and quite entertaining, to watch someone else wrestle with challenges that resembled my own.

In one of my favorite episodes, Kimora was planning a launch event, and both she and her team were sorely taxed. At the height of the frenzy of getting everything done, Kimora's chief of staff melted to the ground, crying "I just can't do it!"

Kimora bent over—mind you, she is six feet tall—and very matter-of-factly said, "You can quit, but then you will be a quitter." Genius! How simple, but how true.

In the years since I first heard these words, I've remembered them whenever a tough day or week or month tempted me to consider walking away from a challenge. I've also adopted this phrase as a great tool for motivating others.

Chapter 6

Nitty-Gritty Innovation

One of my jobs when I was a product manager—and even more so later, when I became a company leader—was to help drive the development of new products, working with scientists and technical experts who find ways to transform good ideas into practical, profitable realities. But the road to successful innovation almost always isn't a straight line.

Like businesses of every kind, family businesses today are under more pressure than ever to be innovative—to develop new products, processes, services, and methods that better serve customers and make our companies more efficient and profitable. The challenge of being innovative is one everyone in business deals with. If anything, it may be more difficult in a family business, where the tendency to cling to familiar processes and "business as usual" can be especially powerful. Nonfamily businesses can of course be change- and risk-averse as well. In family businesses, however, the emotional charge contained in a *family* culture may result in a context in which making change happen can be challenging.

As a family business leader, I've found it imperative to develop new attitudes and, with those, new processes and new drives to keep our team hyper-focused on what is possible, what is available, and what we can create—and to make sure we are always ready to partner with anyone, anywhere, who can help us grow our business in a powerful new way.

In 2004, our development team was discussing the product category of prophy paste. Prophy paste is that special "toothpaste" that your oral hygienist uses at the end of your appointment to give your teeth a final polish and that great, familiar, dentist-clean feel.

Premier had a prophy paste already, but we were looking for something new. At the time, Life Savers was selling a popular candy called Crème Savers. We decided to create a prophy paste that would mimic Crème Savers in look and flavor, right down to the swirl design. Nothing like this existed. We figured it would be a home run.

We developed prototypes. Then, to test the response of potential customers, we conducted focus groups with dental hygienists. To our dismay, they shot the idea down. "I'd never buy this product," was the common response. "Why would I want to rub candy onto my patient's teeth?"

Of course, we explained that it wasn't candy, it just looked and tasted like candy. But we didn't really change anybody's mind.

When a new idea that you've created and that you love comes into contact with customers for the first time, it can be tempting to ignore or overrule any negative feedback you may receive. There are plenty of excuses you can make:

> "They didn't really get the idea—we just have to explain it better."
>
> "These people don't represent the average customer—I bet real customers will love our product!"
>
> "Plenty of successful products got bad reviews at first—all we need to do is to tweak our idea a little."

Most of the time, however, it's wiser to listen to what the marketplace is trying to tell you. That's what we did in the case of our prophy swirl. After the focus groups, we accepted the fact that what we'd thought would be a huge product had no legs.

So now what?

The answer came out of another team meeting. Our head of research and development reminded us that he'd been working with experts at the National Institute of Standards and Technology (NIST) on a new remineralizing technology. It was a combination of calcium and phosphate salts that could strengthen teeth by reintroducing these enamel building blocks into the tooth surface. It was called amorphous calcium phosphate, or ACP for short. "I bet this ACP could work well in a prophy paste," he said.

We got excited about the idea and decided to contact the NIST people to discuss it further. When we called them about the ACP technology, however, they apologetically informed us that they'd already licensed it to Church & Dwight, a major consumer products company that owns brands like ARM & HAMMER and Waterpik. That meant we probably had no shot at using it.

I wasn't deterred. "Let's call Church & Dwight," I said. "What's the worst that could happen?" In the wise words of my grandfather, "Ask for the order. The worst they can say is no." But they could say yes!

I made the call. That started the ball rolling. I spent months building a relationship with Church & Dwight. We spent that time developing a licensing agreement on a technology that no one else in the market had and discussing a potential partnership in which we would co-brand the product, develop and disseminate educational materials for professionals, and take advantage of other possible synergies. This was possible because each company recognized the potential to build a market, exploit the innovation around ACP, and ultimately bring better oral health to consumers (patients).

With this understanding as our foundation, we both brought our strengths and capabilities to the project, and we devised and implemented our strategies together.

Our negotiations included several meetings with the executives of Church & Dwight at their headquarters in New Jersey, leading up to a meeting in which we finalized the terms of the deal. It represented a major breakthrough for Premier. Our co-licensing deal with Church & Dwight was the first such deal between a consumer products company and a professional dental company, plus our product would be co-branded—an exciting first.

Obviously, I was thrilled. But there was a painful twist to the story coming—one that illustrates one of the toughest parts of working in a family business.

After the meeting, I got into the car, and called my father to tell him the amazing news. I hoped for warm congratulations and maybe an expression of parental appreciation and pride.

Instead, he said, "I don't know if this is such a great idea. This is a brand-new product, we'll have to develop it from scratch, and we're going to have to sell a lot of it to make our investment back."

I felt deflated and pissed. "Yes," I said. "We will have to sell a lot of it. But that's what we do. There's nothing to change now—nor would I. The deal is basically done." I didn't give him any further chance to try to talk me out of it.

The ensuing product changed the trajectory of our business. It proved that we could not only develop unique products through patented technologies, but that we could do so successfully with major players as our partners. Our prophy paste, Enamel Pro, does look and taste like a candy swirl—it's still the only product out there with those features. It comes in flavors like VanillaMint and Mixed Berry—and it's a leader in its category, despite the competition it faces from multibillion-dollar companies like Dentsply Sirona and Envista Holdings.

Of course, not every innovation project works out so well.

Through our licensing and launch of dental products based on ACP technology, we became the pioneers and champions of remineralization in the professional dental space. It gave us strong market share, focus, and expertise in this realm both in terms of technology and education. We decided to capitalize on this. We would develop two new products, a toothpaste and a gel.

We projected them to be two of the biggest projects we had ever launched. After all, we knew the technology. We knew how to sell it. We would figure out how to make it, and we would prove its efficacy. What could go wrong?

As it turned out—*a lot*.

We did create and launch the ACP-based toothpaste and gel. In scientific terms, they were the best products we ever developed and the best products relative to their competition. They could do everything! Usually, toothpastes and gels can do one or two things. Our offerings delivered it all. They included ACP with its remineralizing capability, reduced tooth sensitivity, helped with dry mouth, and even offered greater fluoride uptake than any other product on the market despite actually containing less fluoride.

All of that was the good news. But the bad news was that our products couldn't be manufactured as easily as we anticipated, and they took us six years and hundreds of thousands of dollars to create. And when the products finally hit the market, with their undeniable efficacy and clinical superiority, guess what happened?

No one cared.

In retrospect, some of the mistakes we made were very clear. We developed the product largely through our R&D department, failing to get input and suggestions from our sales and marketing people. We ended up creating perfection—ideal for R&D but, in this case, not for the market. There is a phrase in the world of development: *Don't let the perfect get in the way of excellent.* This time, we didn't do that. Ultimately, the sales of our ACP-based toothpaste and gel did not meet our projections. Lessons learned. In the wake of this failure, we were disciplined. We developed new processes ensuring that we would involve more areas of the company at the outset of development, and studied the market more carefully to make sure we were offering features that customers really wanted rather than ones that, although awesome and scientifically advanced, we simply assumed they would like. As a result, we would bring products to market efficiently, and with an audience that was ready and excited to buy.

At the same time, sometimes it's not so bad when you fail to be first to market. In the right circumstances, and with the right competitive strategy, that "fast follower" thing can really be true.

At Premier, we conduct a large meeting with our marketing, product management, and sales teams once a quarter. As part of this meeting, we review industry data from a third-party analytic report that shows market shares per category and per product. These meetings generate a lot of valuable insights. We see how we are doing relative to our competition, we uncover trends, and we examine new products that have emerged.

In one such meeting, we saw that there was a new product category featuring a single product from one of our biggest competitors. The category was retraction, and the product was a hemostatic and retraction paste.

To explain in layperson's terms: Let's say that you have a large cavity and need a crown or an implant. In order to create that crown and prepare it for placement, the dentist must "prep the tooth," which often involves shaping and cutting the tooth and taking an impression. While this is happening (sorry, people, here's the reality), there is bleeding, which inhibits the dentist's field of vision. One way to remove the blood is through those plastic straw-like things that rest in your mouth and serve as extractors. However, this is somewhat cumbersome. There are materials that can do this as well, which are known as hemostats. These work in a much more concentrated way, as they are put directly onto the bleeding area. The whole process, known as hemostasis, is done deftly and swiftly by your dentist.

Are you with me so far?

Meanwhile, another area of the mouth that needs to be prepped for the crown is the gum, which needs to be pushed away from the tooth a bit to allow for the seating of the crown. In other words, the dentist needs room to cement the crown in. This process of pushing back the gum is known as retraction. This has typically been done by dipping a cord (a little like a mini version of those braided jump ropes that we had as kids) into a hemostatic liquid, and placing that into the gum. This process works, but it takes multiple steps, and can sometimes be uncomfortable for the patient.

Anyway, in our quarterly meeting, we noticed the emergence of this new product category, and a new product—a paste—that took care of hemostasis and retraction all in one. We thought, *Woah! That is a great idea*. This product would make procedures better, faster, and more comfortable for the patient. Plus, the price point was much higher compared to traditional cord and hemostatic liquid. Of course, this was great from a business standpoint.

We all sat in the meeting talking about how smart this was and how disappointed we were that we hadn't thought of it first.

After the meeting, I went to our head of R&D and told him what we had uncovered. He looked up the new product online, and after examining the description and specifications, he said, "It won't work."

"What do you mean it won't work?"

"It won't work. I was a geologist. The main substrate in this product is a clay, and it's not capable of behaving as intended."

I was surprised, but I believed what I was hearing. He was a scientist, and a brilliant one at that. I trusted his expertise—we all did.

But with each passing quarter, we continued to watch the sales of the new hemostatic and retraction paste steadily grow. When they reached $10 million, which is significant for a dental product, we went back to our head of R&D and asked for his take.

"I get that the product is selling," he told us. "But I still say that the clay substrate they're using can't work as well as it should. It could definitely be made better."

Okay—this message from our ex-geologist was exactly what we needed to hear. Now we could get somewhere. We set off on a development journey to make the material of the product better, with improved retraction properties. We were already the market leader in hemostatic solutions, so we would pair that technology with the superior clay.

We originally planned to use essentially the same delivery system as the competition. Their material came in a capsule and was inserted into a "delivery gun" to release it; we would do the same. But then we realized that we could make an even better delivery system as well. Ours would be a sleek three-millimeter syringe. Due to the properties of the clay, it was able to extrude beautifully, and to place the product perfectly into the sulcus, which is a groove in the gum. Now our product would be better than the competition in two ways, not just one.

We believed we had a winner. There was still only one other product on the market, so there was plenty of room for us. The other product was sold through distribution, as were we. We anticipated that we would not convert that business, as our competitor already had a stronghold. Our strategy would be to steal share from the "direct" companies that were selling cord and hemostatic liquid. This was in fact a larger market, and we believed we could be successful in it.

In 2010, we confidently launched our product under the name of Traxodent.

It turned out that our analysis of the marketplace was wrong—but it was the right kind of wrong! We ended up taking *both* the distribution market and the direct market. Traxodent is now the global number one product in its category.

So, yes, being a fast follower can work brilliantly, so long as you know what you are doing. In this example, we recognized the opportunity quickly because we had already established a system for monitoring and studying the marketplace regularly. That enabled us to spot the trend and the competing product before it had built a lead too big for us to overcome.

Then we followed up by doing our technical homework. We had an expert on staff (our R&D head) whose background knowledge revealed the potential for creating a new product that could leapfrog the competition in terms of performance. And we weren't satisfied with beating them on one parameter—we took the time and applied the creativity needed to develop an improved delivery system as well, giving customers two great reasons to buy us instead.

Finally, we developed a smart market segmentation strategy that minimized our risk. Targeting the direct market gave us a great shot at establishing our new product without having to fight an uphill battle against an entrenched rival. It worked so well that we ended up sweeping the entire market, not just the specific niche we initially aimed at.

The moral: When a competing company beats you to market with a better offering, fight! Take it as a challenge. You may have lost round one, but rounds two, three, and beyond are waiting for you to seize.

QUOTE UNQUOTE

"The dollar is round." This was one of my grandfather's adages, a Mortonism that people inside and outside Premier have shared and repeated over the years. It's a reminder that money has a way of rolling in and rolling out. It definitely applies to challenges like innovation, when it can be easy to turn on the money spigot in hopes that just a little more investment will push your project over the top and turn an apparent failure into a success. Yes, you have to spend money to make money. But you'd better make sure that there's a clear purpose for every dollar you spend, and a likely payback coming.

Since the dollar is round, you never know when it will bounce your way or roll away, out of sight. So when you are lucky enough to have it, use it wisely, save some of it for tomorrow, and give generously to those in need.

Chapter 7

The Pressure Is On

In 2013, I was named president of Premier—this time for real. It was a proud, exciting day for me. But the excitement soon had to move over to make space for some different emotions.

I immediately recognized that my relationship with the business had changed dramatically. Now the responsibility for the future of Premier was on my shoulders. I might still be my father's daughter, and my father might still want to apply a guiding hand behind the scenes—sometimes welcomed, sometimes more than I liked—but as far as the company's employees and the outside world were concerned, I was now the face of Premier and the person in control of the organization. I had to prepare us to face the challenges of a changing world.

And from what I could see, we weren't there yet. Internally, Premier was what many businesses are—a solid eight-to-four business. People worked standard company hours. As for working on the weekend—sometimes, but not really happening. Certainly nothing wrong, but also no burning drive. This absolutely wasn't due to incompetence or lack of caring—it was simply the culture that had evolved.

In most ways, our culture was and is great—one driven by

collaboration, happiness, and service. One where employees are valued, customers prized, and relationships cultivated. All super important and constantly inculcated. Among that amazingness, from my vantage point, there also seemed to be a lack of pressure, something that actually felt bizarre and unfamiliar to me, especially when faced with an increased pace of change and competitiveness. I've already mentioned that my father stepped into his leadership role at Premier mainly from a strong sense of family duty and not necessarily from a personal passion for business—a quality that I find admirable. Let's not forget, my father is quite capable. He went to Wharton, and Premier was successful under his leadership. With that success, he still maintained a consistently nonconfrontational personal style. Over time, this style became the norm—devoid of urgency—a problem that's not uncommon in family business. There wasn't that push, that tension, required to adapt a business to an evolving world.

I came from a mindset of detail, follow-up, granularity, thanks in part to my less-than-calm personality, and due in other part to the lessons learned from having previously been fired. Ouch; it hurts just to type that! So sitting in meetings where great ideas were shared, but no investigation, schedules, or to-do lists were initiated was very foreign to me. I am queen of to-do lists. In fact, I have often been complimented on the bulleted lists I send to customers after meetings. A very strange source of pride, but still true. So here, I wondered, "How can there not be anything?!" (I'm too Type A to handle that.) Maybe everyone else had it handled and solidly in their heads, maybe they had already done this, or maybe this was just how things were done. Everyone else seemed okay with that approach. I couldn't be.

Once I became president of Premier, I set out to adjust these habits and practices. Shouldn't everyone in business be Type A? Yes. At least part of the time. Altering the way we handled meetings was a relatively easy fix. I established a practice that, during every meeting, as topics were discussed, we assigned an owner and a time frame. Afterward, I circulated notes from the meeting (yes, those bulleted lists) reiterating everyone's responsibilities and my expectations. Then the kicker: I sent out a calendar invite for the next meeting, which also marked the deadline for things to be completed.

The result? Let's put it this way: We gots lotsa meetings! They're all productive and necessary, though! Well, 90 percent of them are, anyway.

As for accountability: This was a big one. A big one because it is important, and a big one because previously it hadn't necessarily been prioritized. Take a situation that all of us are reluctant to do: dismissing people. Obviously, it's important to be judicious in cases of termination. You can harm a company if you fire people when it's not warranted or if you are callous and cruel when you do it. But you can harm a company even more if you fail to remove someone when it's necessary.

We had one situation where an employee admitted to stealing from the company. My father wanted to put him on probation. Yeah, no. There are some behaviors that demand the strongest possible penalty, and stealing is one of them.

So, when appropriate, I fired people. That seemed to be rather jarring. But it sent an important signal to the entire company. It told people that, at Premier, our behavior matters; that we are expected to live up to our commitments to one another and to the organization; and that hard work, integrity, and excellence are part of the deal. It goes back to Mortonism 101: Remember who you are.

Igniting the company culture was at the top of my agenda as president of Premier. But I knew that making it happen wouldn't be easy, and it wouldn't be fast. Shifting a company's culture is a job that you have to be in for the long haul; it's not something you can do overnight or once and for all.

It's also not a painless task. The leader at the top of the organization often has to face some grueling moments in the course of moving a company ahead.

One of the most difficult processes I had to work through during my years as president of Premier were the negotiations involving my eventually being named CEO and the revision of the related corporate governance documents. In the process, my father would relinquish his role as CEO and owner and move into a new status as chairman of the board. The details were complicated and very specific to Premier and the Charlestein family. But the decisions to be made involved a number of questions that many family businesses need to wrestle with at some time—issues like how ownership shares will be divvied up among various members of the family, how those shares will be paid for or otherwise transferred from one owner to another, how important decisions about the business will be made, how long the transition from one generation to the next will take, and more.

As with so many of the important issues involved in running Premier, this required some challenging conversations with my father, which were complicated by our unique relationship and his approach to business. At times, when my father and I were at odds, he would vaguely suggest that he might want to reconsider things we'd already settled, like ownership shares, decision-making authority, and other matters. This made the whole process very stressful for me. My attorney described these negotiations as "like nothing I have ever seen." When a business lawyer with decades of experience says this, you know it's true—and that the process has not been an easy one.

These months of negotiations embroiled me in a period of pain and frustration more intense than any other I've experienced. To give you an idea, I bought a pack of cigarettes even though I don't smoke. (I ended up only smoking one cigarette—a real badass.)

One time in the midst of this period, I found myself in a neighborhood store called Rosenberg's Judaica. I can't remember what I needed to buy. Maybe it was a bar mitzvah gift for someone, a set of Chanukah candles, or a holiday board game to play with my son's class. Anyway, it was something I could buy only at a Judaica store, so there I was one afternoon. Although the store is literally just a four-minute drive from my house, I remember being barely able to get myself there because I was so smothered in darkness by what was going on with the negotiations as well as all the related aspects of my relationship with my father. But I'm a working mother, so I gotsta keep moving.

Rosenberg's is a very small store, probably half the size of your local Starbucks. As you walk in, the wall on your right is lined with Judaic texts. Right in front of you is a selection of kosher wines. To the left of that is a jewelry case with the familiar Magen David and Chai necklaces. Behind that are shelves filled with Jewish-themed books. And the back wall has all of the Shabbos stuff: silver Kiddush cups, ceramic Kiddush cups, intricate Shabbos candle holders, challah boards, challah covers, and challah knives.

That's where I was when I must have hit rock bottom. I say this because I remember passing the Shabbos wall and thinking, "I wonder if I could bring myself to pick up one of those challah knives and jam it in my stomach."

Thankfully I got through that day, and those weeks, without doing any harm to myself (or to anyone else). And in the end, our complex decisions about ownership and control of Premier got resolved amicably and, I believe, for the good of the business. The fact that my father is conflict-averse ended up working in our favor: as the negotiations dragged on, his desire to come to closure grew stronger and stronger, making it easier for us to finally resolve the issues that threatened to divide us.

But if anyone ever tells you that dealing with a family business and its culture is easy, don't believe them.

Of course, not everything about taking the reins at Premier and beginning to change the way the company does business was slow or painful.

It was very important to me both to make my own mark and to "remember who I am" in the context of Premier. To me, this included everything from working hard, taking smart risks, and being innovative, to networking differently. I wanted to begin to create a new, more forward-looking image for Premier that would help position our company as an industry leader.

My husband recognized what I was trying to do and was very supportive of it. He offered me both moral support and, occasionally, ideas that I found really helpful. One of his suggestions was for a small gesture that could help in building relationships and friendships and in solidifying my place within our organization and the industry. It was a simple concept—sending handwritten thank-you notes.

Yes, it's an old-fashioned idea. In fact, it's an art that is virtually lost. Almost no one takes the time to write and send handwritten notes. Everyone sends cursory emails or no message at all. At my husband's suggestion, I decided I would do things differently. So I bought a set of beautiful stationery and began to write.

I wrote a note of appreciation after every meeting or encounter that I had. I wrote with sincerity about the experience that I had had with the individual I was addressing and what it had meant to me. I continue the practice to this day, and I think it has become a signature of my style. I've even kept a collection of samples of each stationery design that I've used, and I plan to paper my office with them one day!

The best of many recognitions of this small habit came when a senior executive from a very large company told me how much he enjoyed getting my notes—and that he keeps them and often rereads them. I like the idea that, just by making a personal connection through the written word, I can make Premier an even more important presence in the life and mind of a valued business colleague. This, too, is part of the corporate culture I'm trying to establish at Premier—something I hope will outlast my years with the company and help to keep it strong and flourishing for generations to come.

As the stories in this chapter show, changing elements of a company culture can sometimes be like driving a sports car. Other times, it's like captaining a yacht. Some of the things that I wanted to transform at Premier were obvious and would react immediately to my efforts, like a sports car that handles curves effortlessly. Others were much more subtle and would move slower, requiring thoughtful and deliberate planning, like a yacht whose course can be changed only gradually. When you need to rebuild your company's culture, try to get clear about the characteristics of each effort you're making, and handle them accordingly.

Chapter 8

An Actor, a Dress Designer, and a Prime Minister Walk into a Bar . . .

If you've participated in your share of corporate team-building exercises or training programs, you've heard most of the traditional icebreaker questions designed to help people get to know one another and open up about their personalities, values, and interests:

> "If you were going to be stranded on a deserted island, what three possessions would you want to take with you?" (Personally, I can't understand why anyone answers this one with anything other than "A shortwave radio, a GPS system, and a high-powered motor boat with a full tank of fuel," but then what do I know?)
> "If money were no object, how would you spend your time?" (Given my Type A personality, it's hard to imagine that I would want to stop working.)

"If you could invite anyone in the world—living or dead,
   real or fictitious—who would you invite to a dinner
   party?"

This third question is the one that excites me the most. Who is on *your* list? I happen to think my list is fabulous:

- Katharine Hepburn
- Diane von Fürstenberg
- will.i.am
- Bethenny Frankel
- Clayton Christensen
- David Ben-Gurion
- Morton Charlestein and Malvina Charlestein

I like this question because my imaginary dinner party is the only chance I'll ever get to bring together all the people who've inspired and motivated me over the years, whose philosophies have inspired mine, and whose examples have helped to shape my thinking and my present perspective.

Yes, I admit it's a weird list. Growing up in the 1970s, *Sesame Street* was of course one of my favorite shows. It still is. I still know all of the words to the theme song. I still remember when Mr. Snuffleupagus (the giant, mammoth-like Muppet who lives in a cave just off Sesame Street) was a figment of Big Bird's imagination. And I still fondly recall breaking into "C is for Cookie" with my own kids when they were little.

Another familiar segment from *Sesame Street* was "One of these things is not like the others"—a game set to a song (called "One of These Things (Is Not Like the Others)") that challenged kids to figure out which thing was different from the others. So you might see pictures of an apple, a hamburger, an ice cream cone, and a mitten . . . and, yeah, the mitten is the one that's different. (Nice guess.)

When I think about the people whose philosophies have had an impact on me, I think of that game. Although when I look at the people gathered around my imaginary dinner table, *none* of these people is like any other. It's as if the choices are a popsicle, a motorcycle, a sneaker, and a duck. Nutty, right?

My list of dinner party guests also reads a little like the setup for one of those old jokes—you know the kind: "An actor, a dress designer, and a prime minister walk into a bar . . ." I just haven't figured out the punch line yet.

But this eclectic mishmash of characters, characteristics, accomplishments, and experiences speaks to who I am.

So, I'll have the chopped salad—dressing on the side—and let me go around the table, introduce you to my guests, and explain why each one is here.

I'll start with the grand lady seated at the head of the table (I wouldn't necessarily put her there, but I have a feeling she'd take that seat without being asked, as if she'd been born to it): Katharine Hepburn.

When I was young, I was virtually unaware of Katharine Hepburn—I'd heard of her, but I really didn't know the first thing about her. She became important to me through one of those almost random events that you might call "accidental" except that, in retrospect, it seems as if it was fated to happen.

My family and I were at my grandparents' house in Florida—a place I'd grown up visiting and where I was now hoping to make similar memories for my children. One day, we were all lazing around in the living room. The kids and I were watching an episode of *Parks and Recreation* (love Amy Poehler—she's on the guest list for my *next* imaginary dinner party). While we watched Leslie Knope concoct some goofy scheme to solve a local government problem, my husband picked up one of the big picture books on the coffee table in front of the sofa. It listed what some group of experts had decided were the one hundred most influential people in the world. Everybody loves lists. So he started leafing through it.

Halfway through the book, Darryl handed the book to me open to a page, and just said, "Read this; it's you."

The page was a tribute to Katharine Hepburn. It featured an amazing photo of her—fashionable, strong, cool. How could this possibly have anything to do with me?

But then I read the quotation alongside the photo: "I have not lived as a woman. I have lived as a man. I've just done what I damn well wanted to, and I've made enough money to support myself, and ain't afraid of being alone."

It left me speechless. My husband was right. That *is* me. That comment might be considered heresy by some women. After all, isn't feminism about having pride in being a woman, and about insisting that living as a woman is every bit as good as living as a man? No matter. Hepburn's message totally resonated with me. It was my being. It encapsulated in a few words what my life has been and how I've positioned myself.

Independence—there's nothing more important to me. It not only means doing things for myself, but being financially independent, free of the need to rely on others. It also means being strong, self-aware, and unapologetic—though admittedly I am still working on that last piece.

The best part of this story is that my husband is the one who showed me the page in the book—in effect, the one who introduced me to Katharine. I don't know many husbands who would be proud that that quote embodies their wife's outlook. Mine is— and I love him for that (among a million other reasons).

My second "ill-fitting" influence is Diane von Fürstenberg, the iconic designer, businesswoman, philanthropist, entrepreneur, and leader. Those who know me might be surprised to have me name a superstar of the fashion world as one of my core influences. No one would ever confuse me with a model or a fashionista. I am impressed with women who always seem to look sharp and put-together; I need help to get there.

When I first met Darryl, he was living in Toronto, and I quickly joined him there. Not having any friends in town, I befriended Lisa, the girlfriend of Darryl's best friend (now one of my close friends as well). Lisa invited me out one night with some of her friends so I could expand my circle. I remember constantly thinking to myself, "Wow, these girls all look so great. Why is that? How do they do it?"

Then it occurred to me: "Oh, they are wearing makeup and cute clothes!"

As you can see, a deep understanding of fashion and how to achieve it was something that I never possessed.

I suppose that I would compare myself to Andy Sachs, the character played by Anne Hathaway in *The Devil Wears Prada*. When she first goes to work for *Runway* magazine, she horrifies her boss, the editor-in-chief played by Meryl Streep, because she doesn't know the difference between cerulean and blue.

So what draws me to Diane von Fürstenberg? The answer is her continuing evolution, her ability to maintain relevance at every stage of her life and career. Daughter to a Holocaust survivor who had been a prisoner at Auschwitz, young Diane learned about fashion as an apprentice to a textile manufacturer in Italy. In 1974, she created her knitted jersey wrap dress, which became a fashion icon comparable to Chanel's little black dress in its lasting influence. By 1979, her company had annual sales of upwards of $150 million.

In later years, she launched other businesses, from cosmetics and jewelry to beach wear; she created a home-shopping business that sold $1.2 million worth of merchandise in two hours on QVC; and she helped build a family foundation that gives millions to causes from human rights to the environment. She even created a reality TV show—an amazing choice for a woman of her success, fame, and fortune. Why take that kind of risk? I'd say it was in order to reimagine herself and to become known to a new generation of women.

Early in her life, Ms. von Fürstenberg said that she didn't know what she wanted to be, but she knew the *type* of woman that she wanted to be. She wanted to be "the kind of woman who is independent and who doesn't rely on a man to pay her bills." She lived by this creed, despite being married in her twenties to Prince Egon von Fürstenberg (a wealthy prince) and in her fifties to Barry Diller (a billionaire media mogul).

I too am driven by the need for independence. But how far will it drive me? Will it drive me to build an empire, and to create a legacy that will serve as an example to my children, and their children, and their children? I like to think it will—but, to be honest, I just don't know. I'm going to keep working as hard as I can for as long as I can, and we'll see what happens then.

Oh, and one more thing I love about Diane von Fürstenberg: She actually looks like my grandmother—a stunning woman who was a model when she was young. Maybe the two of them can share stories about the fashion business when they sit across the table from one another at my dinner party!

I am guessing that Diane von Fürstenberg has sat next to one or two rappers at dinner parties. If so, it's appropriate that the next guest at my party will be will.i.am, the rapper, singer, songwriter, and record producer.

I came to know about will.i.am when he was a founding member and lead singer of the phenomenally successful group Black Eyed Peas. Later I followed his career as a judge and mentor on the shows *The Voice UK, The Voice Australia,* and *The Voice Kids.* As I've mentioned, I never get tired of watching reality TV. But will.i.am's entire life story is an incredible one. He grew up in a housing project in L.A. and dedicated himself to creating a musical career starting while he was in high school. As a member of Black Eyed Peas, and in collaboration with other artists, he has had forty-one hit songs on the UK Singles Chart and has sold millions of records. He has also produced records with artists ranging from Michael Jackson and Justin Timberlake to Britney Spears, U2, Nicki Minaj, and Lady Gaga.

Oh, and I guess I should mention that in 2011 he was named Intel's director of creative innovation; that in 2012 he worked with NASA to become the first artist to stream a song from the surface of Mars; and that he has acquired and helped to run a number of high-tech start-up companies working in fields like machine learning and smart watch design.

When I think about will.i.am, I think about three words: *authenticity, creativity, intellect.* Put those qualities together and you have a unique package. No wonder he is a favorite of mine.

Let's move on to the fourth guest at my dinner table—Bethenny Frankel. If you've heard of her, it's probably because of her eight years as a star of *The Real Housewives of New York City,* as well as her appearances on Martha Stewart's version of *The Apprentice* and several other television series. That would be more than enough for me to invite her to join the dinner party. My obsession with reality TV actually started with the *Real Housewives* shows. I have watched every season of those shows, set in every city. They're my escape, my psychological and emotional treat, the reward I permit myself when traveling for work and I've completed all my tasks for the day. They provide me the total mindless respite I need after hours of tough negotiating and problem-solving.

And if you feel like judging me, first think about your own guilty pleasures! I bet you have some that are just as embarrassing as mine.

So, yes, I love Bethenny for the assertive, honest, and cuttingly funny persona she displayed as one of the *Real Housewives*. But there is more to Bethenny than her TV career. She is also a serial entrepreneur, having launched several businesses, from a short-lived party-planning company to a baking business. Her biggest successes have been her self-help and lifestyle books, especially those built around her Skinnygirl brand of food and beverage products. She is disciplined, unapologetic, relentless in pursuing her goals, and totally self-made—she was estranged from her family, which meant she achieved success without relying on their help. What's not to admire?

For a change of pace, my next dinner guest is Clayton Christensen, a former professor at Harvard Business School. Though he was perhaps best known as the popularizer of the concept of "disruption," Christensen wrote a string of provocative books that have been huge bestsellers and influenced an entire generation of business leaders.

I first got to know him and his work when I read the 2004 book *Seeing What's Next*, which Christensen coauthored with Erik A.

Roth and Scott D. Anthony. What an experience—it was so compelling that I felt as though I should have been sitting in a Southern Baptist Convention church on a Sunday morning, screaming "Hallelujah!" as I read it. Christensen has a unique capacity to use storytelling and science to illuminate the future and tell the rest of us how to anticipate, understand, and prepare for it. Whenever I think back to his writing, I appreciate his prescience, and it inspires me to try to think in the same way.

If I had to name three words to capture Christensen's gifts, as I did with will.i.am, the words I'd choose would be *curiosity, legitimacy, sharing.* I'm so glad I discovered his work.

Sitting next to Dr. Christensen—in case he ever gets tired of chatting with his other table companion, Bethenny Frankel—is that remarkable world figure, David Ben-Gurion. A leader of the Zionist movement, Ben-Gurion helped to write the Israeli Declaration of Independence; was the first person to sign it; and, on May 14, 1948, he formally proclaimed the creation of the modern state of Israel.

The nation was immediately besieged by enemies, and Ben-Gurion played a key role in uniting various independent underground defense units into what became known as the Israel Defense Forces. After achieving a remarkable victory in the 1948 Arab–Israeli War, Ben-Gurion became the first prime minister of Israel, and to this day he is revered as the founding father of his country. He helped build the nation's political and economic institutions; led Israel as it successfully absorbed millions of Jews from around the planet; and forged positive diplomatic relations with most of the world's important powers, including West Germany, with whom Ben-Gurion negotiated a deal to provide reparations for the seizure of Jewish property during the Holocaust.

One can only imagine the fortitude, courage, talent, and tenacity it took for Ben-Gurion to achieve this amazing series of successes—taking a dream that millions had nurtured for hundreds of years and finally turning it into a reality.

The two final guests at my dinner party must be my grandparents, Morton Charlestein and Malvina Charlestein—of course. I've already told you why I admire them so much. They were smart, loving, energetic, supportive, humble, philanthropic, and revered.

I'll continue to mention and quote them in the remaining chapters of this book. But, meanwhile, I hope they have fun at their granddaughter's dinner party. They made it possible.

Whenever I am leading a business meeting, I like to start with a Question of the Day. It's a fun way to get everyone settled and help them know each other a little better. If you'd like to try this in your next meeting, you could ask, "Who would you want to invite to a dinner party?" The answers will give you insights into the personalities and values of the people attending your meeting. More important, it will help each of them to know more about who they are, what qualities they admire, and what they'd like to learn.

Chapter 9

Envisioning a New Premier

The day that I became CEO was April 1, 2016. I expected nothing special. I had been president for three years at that point, so what would be different now?

The answer turned out to be everything. Going into the office that day, the gravity of the change hit me.

Holy shit. This is all on me. This company has been in business for one hundred years—I can't be the one to screw it up. I have over 150 employees relying on me, looking to me, and scrutinizing me. I have a family expecting me to provide for them what generations before us had.

Now what?

Through years of working in various positions throughout the business, I'd already figured out that Premier needed some retooling to be equipped for what was to come, both in the industry and the world. In order to be in business and under one ownership structure for over a century, there had to have been evolutions in the past. The present was no different. We needed some changes. Now that I was CEO, the responsibility for making those happen was completely mine.

One of the big changes Premier needed to make when I took

charge was in the area of branding. It was a need I realized after my husband and I got a couple of dogs—partly to please our kids, who, like most kids, were obsessed with having a pet; and partly to please my husband, who had thirteen different dogs over the course of his own childhood. What I didn't realize beforehand was that having dogs would lead to conversations with our neighbors about their dogs, their groomers, and their choice of poop bags. (Stick with me, I promise this story is going to lead back to Premier.)

I found these dog-centered chats totally boring until one of our neighbors brought over his dog to play with ours. When I asked the requisite "What do you do?" question, he replied, "I'm an endodontist."

Yeehaw! An endodontist is a dentist who specializes in dental pulp, tooth pain, and root canal surgery. Finally, someone that I could actually have a substantial conversation with! Being in the industry, I was sure he would react with understanding and excitement when I told him, "I work in the dental business. My company is Premier."

His actual reaction: a long, silent pause.

"You know, Premier," I said. "We are Traxodent. Triple Tray. Enamel Pro."

His eyes came to life: recognition. Once I mentioned our products, he knew exactly who we were.

Which showed me the problem we had.

Premier was certainly very well known. But it was mostly known by distributors, manufacturers—even university researchers. Our main marketing focus had been on our distribution partners, the direct customers we made our sales to, using a push strategy that encouraged them to pass our messaging and products to the dentists.

What we needed was to supplement that with a pull strategy

aimed at getting the dentists to ask distributors for Premier products, propelling our relevance, our independence, and our relationships.

The next day, I told my colleagues, "Premier needs to become a *branded* company instead of what we now are—which is a company of brands. We need to make Premier into a name that is known not just by distributors but by *everybody* in the industry."

We set about making that happen. It was the first of a cascading series of strategic changes. Making Premier a branded company led to changing the way we thought about markets and made crucial business decisions. Rather than being led by the preferences of our dealer network, as we had been in the past, we had to become responsive to the wishes and needs of our customers—both the dentists who bought and used our products and the patients and consumers whose health and happiness we ultimately served.

This speaks to the current phase in Premier's evolution. As I became CEO, and continued to learn about our company, the industry, and varied industries, I realized that both what we needed and what could eventually serve to differentiate us was data. Being customer-centered meant we needed to become a company of people who analyze the changing markets and pay close attention to what they are telling us, who looked at sales configurations, analyzed territories, and used data-driven technology. This drove a large part of our reorganization strategy, including the creation of brand-new positions that had never been considered before. The goal was to become a data-driven, consumer-led organization.

An important secondary element was that we needed to create new and different processes around bringing products to market.

For the longest time, our marketing consisted of creating one ad and placing it in journals, mailers, and dealer catalogues. There was no targeting, no messaging tailored to various audience, no segmenting of markets. We simply crafted and delivered one message: "Here is the most awesome thing ever. Buy it."

This actually worked really well for a really long time. But inevitably, as the world got more complex and more competitive, this strategy was sure to reach its sell-by date. By the time I became CEO, that date had arrived.

Our product development process was similarly dated. It consisted of our head of R&D—fortunately, an absolute genius—coming up with ideas and running them by me. (Just a reminder: I'm not a dentist, nor a scientist, so what did I know?) Based on his ideas and my feedback, he would develop the products, and then—whenever they were ready, which might have been in a few months or maybe in a few years—we would deliver them to our sales and marketing teams to sell.

A totally winning formula! And it really did work—until it didn't.

Product research based on an n of 2 was inactionable. Launching products without extensive consumer data and pointed marketing messaging couldn't happen, and products unveiled later than originally budgeted was unsustainable.

Our goal of being data-driven and consumer-led meant we absolutely needed to examine these areas of the business and fundamentally change our processes, our timing, and our deliverables, all while creating a culture of performance. Not a quick and easy transition. It required new skills that Premier hadn't previously focused on developing. It opened the door to the next phase in my effort to build a new Premier: yes, a re-org.

After rising to the office of CEO in 2016—solidifying the leadership role I'd assumed with the presidency—I set about making this transition happen. Doing this took quite a bit of courage on my part. Fortunately, I'd been gradually developing the self-confidence I needed to drive the necessary changes.

The story of SmartCaps illustrates how I came to fully believe in myself as a leader and a change agent—and how I applied that new self-knowledge to making things happen at Premier.

SmartCaps is an amazing technology that our head of R&D worked on in partnership with researchers at Creighton University, a major university dental school located in Omaha, Nebraska. Essentially, SmartCaps consists of microcapsules created through a process known as reverse emulsion (details not necessary—well, let's be honest: details unable to be explained with scientific accuracy by the author) that can be filled with various constituents (such as calcium and phosphate or flavors), can be programmed to burst, and are permeable (meaning that the constituents are able to move into or out of the microcapsules). The coolest thing (according to the scientists who have explained it all to me) is that the SmartCaps are rechargeable.

(*Note to the reader:* Chances are that you are not a scientist, a chemical engineer, or a polymer developer. If so, what I have written above may sound very complicated. Don't feel bad—it *is* very complicated, so much so that I barely understand what I just typed. If you *are* a scientist, a chemical engineer, or a polymer developer, I apologize for explaining the field you have devoted your life to in terms resembling the way a preschool teacher explains fingerpainting to the toddlers in her class. I am doing the best I can.)

Anyway, what really matters is why SmartCaps technology is so useful and powerful: If you have a product with SmartCaps in your mouth—a commonly used cement or sealant, for example— and you brush your teeth with fluoridated toothpaste, the fluoride in the paste can essentially migrate into the SmartCaps and, over time, get re-released directly into the enamel—thereby strengthening your teeth.

How cool is that?!

Science.

SmartCaps is an example of how amazing Premier is. We quickly realized that, with this technology, we would be able to create many innovative products that would bring real solutions to dentists and their patients. That's a nice market. Statisticians report that there are about 160,000 dentists in the U.S. and about 700,000 in the world. Obviously, their patients number in the hundreds of millions.

But we also realized that SmartCaps technology could have greater reach if developed not just for use in products applied by dentists in their offices, but for use in a wide variety of consumer products. Think about it: You could have SmartCaps in your toothpaste to release chemicals that will make your teeth stronger. You could have SmartCaps in your moisturizer to make your skin more supple. You could have SmartCaps in your laundry detergent to make your clothes smell nicer, longer. There's *lots* of cool stuff that can be done with SmartCaps, most of them things that Premier is not positioned to do on its own.

So after I learned all about SmartCaps (or as much as my non-technical brain could absorb), I thought, "Hey, let's get this out there. Let's license it to a consumer company that can do what we can't. That will be good for the world, good for our partner company, and great for Premier."

But then I wondered, "What's the next step?" Or, to put it more bluntly: "How the hell do we do that?" I knew that the technology was super-solid, super-valuable, and could be eloquently, deeply, and accurately explained and demonstrated by our head of R&D and backed by the many studies and published articles that we had produced in the course of developing it. But how exactly would we get the idea in front of the consumer company leaders who need to learn about it—some of whom have only a vague idea of who Premier is and why our technology is so fantastic?

Lucky for me, I sat on the board with an executive of one of the world's biggest consumer companies. I decided to ask him for guidance. It was very important to me that I not try to *sell* this technology to him. Instead, I needed to listen and learn. I explained that we had a technology that I thought could benefit his company. I wanted to understand what the standard channels for submission or presentation of a product idea looked like there.

He explained that it basically involved visiting the company's website, clicking on their "new concepts" portal, and then uploading our technology. If it was interesting enough for them to take a closer look, someone would be in touch with us. He also added, "Of course, you understand that we probably get a thousand calls and emails with new product concepts every week. It's extremely rare that any of them leads to a serious conversation—let alone an actual business deal."

I thought, to quote a favorite movie of mine (*Dumb and Dumber*), *So you're telling me there's a chance!*

I explained all this to our head of R&D, and we followed the prescribed process, adding our idea to the pile with the rest. Then we waited. And, unbelievably, we got an email from the consumer company. They wanted to set up a call to learn more.

Aaaahh—this was amazing! Our head of R&D and I synchronized our calendars and wrote an email back offering a few dates for a call. Each of us would have a clear role during that call. Our head of R&D would illuminate the wonders of SmartCaps, and I would talk about Premier and describe the ways that we could work together.

The call was scheduled for April. I remember that because it was Passover and I was with my family in Florida, where we'd planned some work-free time. But I sure as shit was going to make an exception for that call.

I organized my day to guarantee that I could focus on the call with no distractions. This is not an easy thing to do when your kids are little. Like most kids, mine would demand my attention at random, unpredictable times—and explaining that sometimes I didn't have any attention to give them was difficult. I had two favorite go-to lines that I would use in that situation. One was, "Yes, you can see me, but I am really invisible." That sometimes worked. When the situation was even more demanding, I went to number two:

"Only come and get me if it is an emergency—which is defined as flames coming out of your stomach."

On this day in April, I used the "flames coming out of your stomach" line ten minutes before the scheduled call. Then I shut my bedroom door and spent those ten minutes reviewing my notes for the umpteenth time—the research that I had done on the consumer company, its products, and its industry position, as well as the messages I was going to deliver about Premier and how we would be an incredible business partner. I didn't bother to review any of the information about SmartCaps; I didn't need to, since our head of R&D would be on the call.

The time came, and I dialed in. The automated voice of the conference call system informed me, "There are two participants in the call." The executive from the major consumer products company was on the line. I greeted him, introduced myself, and explained, "Our head of R&D will be joining us any minute." The two of us chatted in a friendly way while we waited. We each explained where we were calling from, we exchanged notes about the weather in our separate locales, and we started offering comments about our plans for the spring holidays . . . all while I was getting more and more nervous with every passing moment. I grabbed my laptop and sent a frantic email ALL IN CAPITAL LETTERS DESPERATELY PLEADING FOR OUR HEAD OF R&D TO JOIN THE CALL. But more minutes passed, and the beautiful beep that would tell us that a third party was coming on the line never came.

I finally realized that I was on my own. *Fuuuuuuck!*

So I began to explain SmartCaps—what it was, how it worked, how it had been developed, what it could be used for, how it could be produced and marketed. The executive from the consumer company listened and asked questions. All the while, of course, I was sweating profusely—and not because I was in Florida.

But ten minutes into the conversation, something strange happened. It suddenly occurred to me that *I was actually answering the executive's questions, and he was understanding and liking my responses.* We were having a real, science-and-technology-based discussion, and I was holding my own. Insanity!

The conversation wound down. I gave my best pitch about the brilliance of Premier, the quality of our people, and our century of excellence (all true, and the parts of the presentation that I could have done in my sleep), and I waited nervously to hear the consumer executive give some kind of overall response to our idea.

Finally, there was a natural pause in the discussion, and the executive commented, "This has been a great conversation. The

SmartCaps idea is very interesting. I think there's real potential for a partnership here. I plan to share what I've learned with the other members of my team, and we'll get back to you with next steps."

Whaaat—he came to *that* based on what I'd said? No fucking way!

But yes way. The consumer company got back in touch, and since then we have been testing and developing SmartCap solutions with them. Go me!

I never found out the reason why our head of R&D had missed the call. (I never asked him because I was seriously annoyed.) I forgave him, of course, with the understanding that if it ever happened again, I reserved the right to personally disembowel him in front of the entire Premier workforce.

I would never wish a nerve-wracking experience like this on any other business leader. This is *not* the way that meetings crucial to the future of your company should go.

But I'm not sorry it happened. In fact, it's one of my favorite career moments. That phone call left me knowing, for the first time, and once and for all, that I'm truly a peer of my counterparts at any company in the world—that I'm capable of doing anything they can do and, in some cases, more.

That's an amazing, exhilarating thing to realize. And when it happens to you—which I hope it will—you'll discover that it's a turning point in your life.

At this point, the story of SmartCaps was just beginning. We have since gone to on to spend three years—1,095 days, also known as a long time—working with this oral care partner on getting the technology ready for widespread adoption.

That, my friend, is very serious business. The steps involved in such a partnership are numerous and complicated. There's the initial explanation of the technology, the sharing of the patents, the discussing with the developers. Then live meetings at their headquarters, which turned out to be not intimidating at all! Everyone there was dressed like they work at Wawa, yet they all had PhDs. One of the guys was actually the developer of one of the most successful consumer products in the country, something you've heard of and probably even used (but which, in the interests of confidentiality, I will *not* name).

Of course, when creating business partnerships, the personalities also have to match. That is not a worry with the Premier team. Everyone is awesome! I hire them to be that way. One of the most important things that I look for in an executive, aside from the obvious skill set needs, are humility and a true sense of genuineness. So whenever we meet with anyone, no matter how intimidating, we shine. (Although maybe I am the only one intimidated by the brilliance of people from other companies. The PhDs and DDSs on our team probably aren't. They're my muscle.)

Bringing the Premier team to work in the lab of a giant company felt like a triumph in and of itself. From there, the work kept going. The technology had to undergo a vetting process that was *insane*. In vitro testing, calcium release tests, phosphate release tests, fluoride uptake tests, calcium and phosphate combined release tests, calcium release in a neat gel, phosphate release in a neat gel, release in gel with flavoring, presence of calcium and phosphate in reservoirs . . . Each of these tests required its own separate protocols. We had check-in calls every few months to review the results of the tests, develop the upcoming ones, and discuss next steps. After every meeting, I sent a meticulous bulleted list of follow-up items, mostly to keep everything straight for myself. I was the only nonscientist involved, and if I didn't immediately digest the information and put it in writing, there would be absolutely no hope for me. I like to think that my notes kept the rest of the team on task as well (wishful thinking).

These vetting tests happened over the course of three years. And with every test, our technology killed it. *Woo-hoo*!

Then it was onto the ultimate test: in vivo, which in this case meant in the mouth. Obviously this required even more vigorous protocols, involving both safety and regulatory departments and oversight. Since this technology was already being used in Premier's dental products, we of course had all of the supporting documentation including safety and efficacy data, 510(k) clearances provided by the Food and Drug Administration, and more. We also had overall literature support for related technology and constituents. So all was approved and we were good to go. Amaze-balls!

The in vivo tests were launched. Ten people would use our product twice a day, and the results would be measured at various intervals using the partner company's own series of tests and protocols. (Remember that I am not a scientist, so, if you are, please accept my apologies for my crude explanations.)

This series of tests took the longest. And again, we nailed it! Our technology proved to over-deliver on the anticipated results. I was thrilled. This is what we've all been looking for and waiting for, right? Let's talk business terms—licensing, production, royalties, all of which I consider the fun stuff.

But no. I learned there was one more hurdle to get over: regulatory and safety testing based on the commercial regulations of various countries. In particular, we had to test the biodegradation of the capsules in waste water. To meet the regulatory standard, this biodegradation needed to take place within thirty days. (To explain: SmartCaps technology consists of teeny-tiny capsules that are permeable and allow for calcium, phosphate, and other constituents to pass through them. The capsules themselves are composed of polyurethane. The next test was to determine how long it takes for these capsules to break up in waste water.)

The test is known by the name OECD 301B. It just sounds menacing, doesn't it?

I discovered that this test was in some ways the toughest test of all. In fact, our head of R&D explained that the possibility of our technology degrading to meet the standards of the OECD 301B test was highly unlikely. Not what I wanted to hear. But science is science. She did say, however, that some bacteria have been found to degrade polyurethane. If we could run a separate test with the addition of those bacteria, there was an outside chance that we could get the intended result.

Again, I trotted out my movie line: *So you're saying there's a chance!*

That became our new motto. Every time we spoke about the test and discussed the long odds against succeeding, I would say, "So you're saying there's a chance!" I even sent our R&D head a YouTube clip of that scene from *Dumb and Dumber*.

But this biodegradation test is turning out to be our nemesis. We ran the OECD 301B test and found—as expected—that our polyurethane did not degrade in waste water. We also asked our partner company whether we could run a variant with other bacteria present. Their answer: No. *Aaaah!*

Science is science. Now we are looking at reformulation to get past the final barrier. This science shit is rough!

QUOTE UNQUOTE

"Enough! Follow me!" I said these words while visiting one of Premier's manufacturing facilities—a factory that had been run by most of the same management team since the 1980s, and that hadn't been modernized in all that time.

I hired Stefan, a sharp German consultant, to study the operation and suggest improvements. He did this—but when I attended the meeting where he presented his ideas, I heard every proposal being stubbornly rejected. No matter what Stefan suggested, the members of the Premier team had some excuse as to why it wouldn't work, why they could never implement it, or why it didn't apply to Premier's unique production methods.

Basically, all these messages boiled down to the same thing: "We're comfortable doing things the way we've always done them, and we have no intention of changing."

When I'd listened long enough to Stefan's presentations and ideas being summarily dismissed, I loudly declared, "Enough! Follow me!" and led the whole team from the conference room to the factory floor, where I pointed to an old machine covered with dirt and grease.

"I don't know anything about manufacturing," I said, "but I know our equipment, even the outdated, shouldn't look like this!" From that moment on, my team paid attention to Stefan—and to me.

Making change happen in an organization is never easy. Overcoming internal resistance takes vision, clarity, empathy, patience, and persistence. But eventually, a moment comes when a leader needs to say, "Enough!" and lead the troops over the barricades. Look for that moment, and be prepared to take advantage when it arrives.

Chapter 10

From Vision to Reality

I like to think I know everything. But that's not the case.

When I took over as CEO, I had my vision—for Premier to become a data-driven, consumer-led company. I had the strategy and a picture of what we needed to be. But I didn't know the exact details as to how to execute.

Working out those details turned out to be a big job in itself. You always hear stories about amazing business plans, ideas, or inventions being hatched on a napkin at a restaurant. Maybe that works for simple concepts—for example, the Laffer Curve, the idea behind the tax cuts implemented by the Reagan administration, which was supposedly sketched on a napkin at a Washington, D.C., restaurant by economist Arthur Laffer. (The original napkin is now on display at the Smithsonian Institution.) Hey, that was just about changing the management of the entire U.S. economy—no big deal! Not like figuring out how to transform Premier Dental Products.

In my case, I used reams of paper to sketch ideas for our new organizational structure. Drafts and drafts and drafts. At one point, I worked on them at a restaurant near our offices in Philadelphia with a very close friend and trusted advisor. He helped me to condense my vision, concentrating on the roles that Premier needed, not on specific people, thereby setting up an ideal structure for our company's success. Sometimes it's incredibly helpful to enlist a smart outsider to help you think about the future of your business. A person with no direct relationship to your company and with no skin in the game can provide an outside perspective that helps you see things you might otherwise overlook. My friend also helped me maintain my focus on the big picture rather than getting lost in the weeds—which is easy to do when you're juggling so many moving parts at once.

The biggest transformational challenge Premier faced was finding the right people to turn the vision into on-the-ground reality.

You know the saying: "Know what you don't know." If you *don't* know what you don't know—or worse, if you're firmly convinced that you are an expert about things you actually are ignorant about—you and your organization are probably heading for a world of pain.

I try hard to recognize my own blind spots so that I can address them with insights and knowledge from the people around me. I know that I can devise a strategy, lead, and inspire. I also know that I *don't* know how to design and implement a system for customer relationship management (CRM), how to deeply analyze sales data, or how to develop a marketing automation process. Which means that, to transform Premier, I needed to hire people with all these skills and more.

This would also mean evaluating the best placements for people who were part of the current organizational structure, moving them as necessary, as well as creating new roles and correctly placing individuals in those roles. I created several new positions: a chief marketing officer (CMO), a director of strategy, and later a director of project and relationship management. I had some ideas about who should go where, as well as the caliber of people that I needed to hire to enhance our organizational capabilities. Additionally, there were a few members of the senior team who would be retiring, so I needed to find their replacements, and, ideally, hire them with some overlap so that the transitions would be as seamless as possible (and, let's face it, so that I wouldn't have to do most of the training).

These various activities on the human resources front all happened simultaneously, which made for a busy, stressful time. Every company likes to say, "Great people are our most important resource." It's true—and at Premier especially so. But how does that translate for the company CEO trying to fill these roles?

In my case, it meant spending two years with half of my time devoted to being a talent scout—including looking in some unexpected places. If you've ever been in a leadership position, you realize that that translates into A Shit Ton of Time.

It was also a huge investment of *energy*. But it was worth it. These were the people who were going to be my inner circle, the ones who would shape the new Premier with me. Of course, I made a few mistakes, mostly in cases when I didn't have a clear enough direction around a specific role. However, they were my mistakes, which meant each one was a step up the learning curve for me, helping me to make a better decision with the next personnel choice.

I cast a wide net. I hired people from really large companies—much bigger than Premier—and from outside our industry. I wanted these types of people for their perspectives and their proven energy and drive. They in turn were attracted by the idea of coming to a smaller company where they wouldn't be siloed into a narrow function and would have a chance to make a meaningful impact on an entire organization.

I wrote about some of the personnel choices I made in the introduction to this book. Some of them were outside-the-box picks, including Penny, our vice president of sales, who had worked at AmerisourceBergen despite the fact that, on paper, she had few of the attributes I thought I needed in the job. She has ended up doing amazing work in this new role.

In the end, our executive team ended up being completely transformed. Few people remained in place from the start of the big reorganization. This really was a new Premier—starting with a new cast of characters featuring fresh thinking, a world of diverse experiences, and bold ideas.

Of course, sometimes translating my vision of the new Premier into daily reality was easier said than done.

Yes, I am the boss; I am in charge. That being said, it is rare for me to overtly assert my position. I do not lead by consensus, but I also do not feel the need to remind people that I am the CEO. So if you work for me, you need to be aligned, and sometimes challenge me as well. You need to move the vision forward collaboratively and bring your absolute best every time. You need to have fun, bring new ideas, and love Premier. So far, I'm not disappointed.

I try not to be heavy-handed about the way I lead. My leadership style is enmeshed with humor. Even in difficult situations, laughter will make its way into our meetings. Although this philosophy was definitely tested one year during budget season.

"Budget season"—now there's a phrase that sends terror through people's hearts. Everyone hates it; there really is no more to say. If you've been there, you know. But it's an unavoidable part of the management process that we simply have to get through—and doing it right can make all the difference as to how successful our year is going to be.

Before this particular budget season, I led many meetings where we discussed the numbers for the upcoming year. I made it clear that, due to the challenging economic conditions, our approach would be guided by the principle of "zero-based budgeting." Essentially, I would insist on getting a justification for each budgeted dollar. We would analyze every function for its costs and benefits. We would *not* simply say, "Okay, we spent $5.00 on paper clips last year, so this year we'll plan on spending $5.10." And we would *not* exceed the spending from the previous year unless there was a real reason to do so.

In other words, our budget would be data-driven and projection-led. Not unreasonable.

I knew that this was absolutely the right decision, but I still felt a hint of insecurity around it. Not because I was concerned about whether we could reach our goals, but rather because I was concerned about whether my leadership team would fully embrace the concept.

I was particularly worried because this was the first budget season for several of the new leaders I had hired. As I mentioned, several were seasoned executives from very large companies—and when I say "very large," I mean *huge*. What would they think about this budgeting strategy? Would it make them scrutinize the budgets they were managing and draw an unfavorable comparison to the much larger sums they were used to working with? I found myself lying awake at night and worrying about this for a while, before telling myself, "You're overthinking this—of course there were times when they had to stick to level or even reduced budgets, no matter where they came from."

Finally, the day came when everyone had submitted their proposed departmental budgets for the coming year. One morning, I sat down with our CFO to see how the numbers were looking. My expectation, of course, was that everyone had come in with justified and level (or nearly level) expense figures as requested. That was true—except for two department heads. One had come in with expenses $1.2 million over the total from the previous year, and one at $700K over.

Are you fucking kidding me!

I asked my CFO whether I had communicated my expectations clearly and often enough.

"Yes, absolutely," he said.

Okay, now I was annoyed. I was irritated because my request had been blatantly ignored. Yet along with my passion, I was insecure, wondering how these new team members viewed Premier and our resources. Above all, I needed resolution, which meant every department adhering to the requirement that I had originally mandated: zero-based budgeting, with an eye on keeping the overall dollar volume the same. My instinct was to immediately call each of the "guilty" parties, ream them out for ignoring me, and give them a deadline of a few hours to fix things.

Correctly, I decided against this. *My goal is to lead, not to insist on being right,* I told myself. *I know that I am right, they know that I am right. I just need to explain this in a direct yet humorous way. A way which will achieve my goal of effective leadership and meeting the budget that I want, but without shattering my relationship with the executives.*

I slept on it. (Sometimes, when your emotions are running high, letting a day pass before you act can be the best possible strategy.)

The following day, I called the two execs to meet with me in our CFO's office. The conversation was short. "I'm not that amazing at math," I said, "but I know that $1.2 million is more than zero, and that $700K is more than zero. That's correct, right?" I added with a smile. "Then fix your budgets, and get them back to our CFO by the end of the week."

We all laughed and left the office. The neutral budgets were submitted the next day.

Translating a strategic vision for your organization into concrete reality involves getting hundreds of details right—some big, some small.

I recently had occasion to review our marketing messaging. I realized that our ads were all way too long and wordy and not engaging enough. I brought this to the attention of our marketing and advertising teams who agreed, challenging them to reimagine how and what we were communicating. I set a date at four weeks out for them to come up with a new approach.

When the date for the follow-up meeting arrived, I was hoping to see some new ads with copy that was short, punchy, and memorable. Instead, the new ads were just slightly tweaked—basically, instead of being three paragraphs long with four sentences in each paragraph, they were three paragraphs long with *three* sentences in each paragraph.

"Hulloh, what's the difference?" I asked.

Amidst the nods and chuckles, we talked through my concerns again, and I reiterated even more clearly what should be accomplished. Now the materials are being reworked with passion and excitement from the team. Moral: The expectations always need to be asserted—and sometimes reasserted. Plus, our team did it. We now have awesome new messaging and ads, even iconography. The real lesson: pictures! People don't like to read.

That's just part of being a leader.

While dealing with these kinds of realities, every leader has their own style for communicating with their people and making sure the overarching vision is being followed. Whatever your style is, make sure you apply it consistently and firmly—because if the details aren't in place, the big picture isn't going to turn out the way you planned.

QUOTE UNQUOTE

"It's got to be on legal!" These are the words my assistant told me in 2019, after I'd largely completed the major reorganization of Premier—a three-year job that had required intense study of market dynamics, deep analysis of our company's strengths and weaknesses, and a strategic examination of our needs for the future. Having made a series of crucial changes to prepare Premier for the years to come—adding key people, creating new departments, establishing stronger links among processes and functions—I'd created a new organization chart that was dramatically different from the one I'd inherited.

How different? I discovered that when I asked my assistant to print out two documents—the 2016 organization chart and the new one from 2019. She came back into my office a few minutes later, all apologies. "I can't print out the 2019 chart on ordinary paper like the 2016," she said. "It's got to be on legal!" That was the moment when I realized that the changes I'd been implementing were truly significant.

Chapter 11

Not Just Another Day at the Office

Let's be real: The concept of achieving work/life balance is basically bullshit. For a female CEO in a family business, doubly so.

I had just returned from twenty-four hours in Las Vegas for a sales meeting. Of those twenty-four hours, two to three were spent in the airport on calls discussing the legal strategy and implications for an employee that seemed to have ghosted his job. (Yes, this is a thing that happens—who knew?)

I reached home, exhausted and hungry, at 11 PM on June 24. I had to be on the road at 6 AM the following morning to drive my son to scuba diving camp in Virginia from our home in Philadelphia. I know the dates so clearly because June 25 happens to be my birthday. The schedule of events did not add up to my dream birthday, but I figured that a road trip with my husband and son would actually be fun. I had two preplanned phone calls to make, but that's not bad—two calls in eleven hours on the road. The rest of the time we could relax, chat, and catch up on some episodes of *Parks and Recreation*, right?

Wrong!

For the first two hours of the drive, from six to eight, there was some fun family bonding. I believe my son indulged me in a round of the Alphabet Game. (For the uninitiated, this is a travel game that involves scanning the road signs, license plates on passing cars, signs of buildings, and so on, looking for the letters of the alphabet in order from A to Z. The first one to Z is the winner. Q and J are always the toughest letters to find.) After this, Maccabi got on his phone to watch *The Avengers* superhero movie he had downloaded for the trip.

At eight, our office is ready for business, so I checked in to see how everything had gone with the ghost employee after we executed the plan of action that I'd helped to devise the previous day. I was amazed to learn that none of the steps that we had mapped out had been acted upon. Why not? How do we make sure that this did not happen again? It took multiple calls—none of which I should have had to participate in—to answer these questions and get our action plan back on track.

Note to self: *I see now that it was a mistake for me to get involved in this issue. This is something that I need to work on: figuring out when to be involved in nitty-gritty problems, and when to step back.*

Meanwhile, I had to break away for a time to join my other preplanned call, this one regarding an issue that we were having with one of our suppliers. As I was on the vendor call, I realized that this was maybe another issue for which I shouldn't necessarily be leading the response.

Note to self: *Reread previous note to self.*

Once I was finally finished dealing with the two mini-emergencies that I shouldn't really have been involved with, the day's *real* emergency erupted. I received a series of calls and emails informing me that a newly hired executive was ghosting as well.

(Okay, now I really need to know when the heck this became a thing!) Many people within the organization were finding that he couldn't be reached, which was quite annoying, especially considering that we were in the throes of several product launches—one very major—with which this executive was supposed to be involved.

This crisis *did* require my attention. Was the missing executive okay? If not, who could step in to fill his shoes? If he was okay, what are the parameters for allowing him to return? And had I made a mistake in hiring this person in the first place? Were they a fit? Answering these questions took up several of our hours on I-95.

Then of course I had all of the standard emails that needed attention.

At various points, Maccabi got off of his device, and I explained to him briefly the business problems I was dealing with. I felt that served several valuable purposes. First, it allowed him to be involved—to feel like a true participant in my life. Second, it showed him the importance of what I do and helped him understand the reasons why I can't always be involved with him. Third, it gave him the opportunity to think holistically and analytically about business challenges. (He always asks very pointed and smart questions, and sometimes he even offers great insights and thoughts for me to consider.)

And fourth and most important, it stopped him from playing *Fortnite*, at least for a few minutes!

Nonetheless, recapping the day's activities just now reveals a picture that is not very satisfying. Essentially, I drove from Pennsylvania to Virginia and back in one day—a day that was supposed to be fun and carefree, but ended up being completely stressful, frustrating, and disappointing.

Note to self: *I need to do better.*

The first week of summer break is the worst. Kids are out of school, but nothing else has started yet—no camps, no baseball, no volunteer work, no trips with the grandparents. Just time that needs to be filled by us parents. We have to come up with some kind of entertainment, activities, and supervision. Yes, this is essentially our job, but during the school year, our work is supplemented with school and extracurricular activities. During the summer, it's all on us—and especially during that first, horrendous week.

On the particular day I am recalling, Maccabi had finished tenth grade, and was waiting to start his sushi apprenticeship. Somehow, some way, Maccabi had started watching YouTube videos about sushi: the history of sushi, sushi preparation, fish varieties in sushi, sushi in Japanese culture—you name it, he'd watched it. Obsessed, he began following chefs that he admired on Instagram and other social media sites, and then started to DM them to ask whether he could work for and learn from them.

Unbelievably, they all said yes. My son was thrilled, and I was amazed by his initiative and drive. So began a series of sushi apprenticeships, the latest of which was due to start in a few days.

But today, he was with me at the office. The reason was that he had another sushi meeting scheduled at an amazing restaurant, named Blue Fin, which was close to Premier. So while waiting for his meeting, I was working, giving Maccabi a front row seat. It was actually the first time that he had been with me at my office on a work day.

He picked the right day. It was nuts. There was meeting after meeting, call after call, with emails and texts in between. There were people who needed to see me, legal strategies that needed to be developed, and I was pretty stressed—a few of the things that I was concentrating on had major implications. So—I'm not gonna lie here—there may have been a few yells of frustration throughout the day. Not aimed at anyone, just directed out into the universe from the confines of my office, with no one but Maccabi to hear me. I like to believe that some well-timed private yells are helpful in times of frustration, though I can't say I've ever noticed any true benefits from them.

This went on for the entire morning. My son was very respectful, not trying to talk to me amidst the stress. Every hour or so he would offer to get me water or to replenish the peanuts and Good & Plenty that I have in my office (strange combo but good—gives you a bolt of energy). Every once in a while, I would briefly explain to him what I was working on. It was a great opportunity to cultivate his interest in and knowledge of business and for him to see his mom in action as the dynamic business leader I am. Honestly, it was a chance most kids would love to have. (Okay, maybe I'm deluding myself.)

Finally, it was time for the drive to Blue Fin. (Actually, it was ten minutes late, but on a day like this, that counts as being ahead of schedule.) I packed up for the drive, naming aloud the items I needed as I stuffed them in my bag: "Work pad, highlighter, legal documents, phone numbers for today's calls, list of tomorrow's meetings," and so on. Once the litany was complete, I turned to my son.

"Now do you see—" I began.

And before I could finish my thought, he said, "Why I don't want to work here—yeah."

Note to self: *Oy! Maybe I can do a better job with that cultivation.*

Then there are those days when the routine challenges of juggling business and family get multiplied by ten.

At work one day, I got the dreaded call from my kids' school. The conversation started in the classic way: "This is the school nurse—everything is fine . . ."

This kind of call really infuriates me. If everything is so fine, why are you calling me? Most of the time, everything really *is* fine in the end—but meanwhile I've had a little mini-heart attack and wasted part of my day. But of course I had to ask the nurse, "What's the matter?"

"Your daughter is in tremendous pain," she said. "She has her period, and her tampon is bothering her."

Really, this is why you are calling me? I told the nurse to instruct Ruby to go to the bathroom and remove the tampon.

"Your daughter is inconsolable. She's sitting here in my office and practically hyperventilating."

I sighed, cleared my afternoon schedule, and took the thirty-minute drive to Ruby's school. I found my whimpering daughter on the sofa in their nurse's office, surrounded by her middle school girlfriends. When she saw me, Ruby's whimpers became full-on sobs.

Not being tolerant of these antics, I was unsympathetic. I took Ruby to the bathroom, where she became even more panicky, almost frantic.

"The way to solve the problem," I told her gently, "is to remove the tampon." But she refused to do it.

"The alternative," I explained, "is that I'll have to do it for you."

"Okay," she sniffled.

Really—is this what it has come to? Apparently so!

Feeling like the intake officer at a federal prison, I instructed my daughter to remove her clothes. I gave her one more chance to take care of the problem, but she was still quietly sobbing.

Time was up. So, like someone ripping a Band-Aid off the leg of a wriggling, hysterical child, I did what any loving mother would and yanked out the tampon.

I washed my hands, hugged my daughter (who was relieved and grateful), and went back to the office.

And when I am asked about the unique challenges of being a female CEO . . . need I say more?

How many lives are you responsible for? How many of those lives do you need to orchestrate? How many of those lives need your attention on a daily basis, and to what level?

For me, the answer to the last question is three. Yes, there are many more lives that I am responsible for, starting with our employees at Premier and their families. Those, however, do not require my daily oversight and involvement. The lucky people who get that are my husband and kids.

The fact is that there is probably more that needs to get done and coordinated in my household in a day than in my business. At Premier, to a degree, most days are as anticipated: there are projects to work on, time lines to follow, analyses to be done. At home, every day is different. Monday is tennis, except if there is tutoring for the ACT—but there is tutoring for the ACT only if someone is available to drive my daughter to the lesson. Tuesday is archery, unless there is a large homework project. But archery is an hour away—how does that tie in with everyone else's needs? That's to be determined on an ad hoc basis. Wednesday is the math tutor, unless of course I have a business meeting and can't take the kids to the tutor and my husband is also working late. Thursday is rehearsal for the school play, unless the director cancels it, and then how do the kids get home?

And oh, by the way, has anyone bought food, walked the dogs, or done the laundry?

It's all seemingly impossible to keep straight. But I have developed a system. I call it Talk Day. At the end of every day, usually after dinner and during the first homework break, I call everyone into the main family room and announce, "Okay—let's Talk Day."

At that point, everyone reminds everyone else about the various activities they have scheduled for the next day. Then we figure out how each of those will get accomplished while not disturbing anyone else's schedule.

(Sometimes I question myself about this. Why am I being so accommodating? I'm freaking the fuck out with stress, but I have to make sure that my daughter is driven to an afterschool activity either by me or by my husband. Why! Well, that's our system. Your mileage may differ.)

Once everyone's activities and designated responsibilities have been established, we all go on with our night—studying, work, watching *The Real Housewives*. The next morning, we each do our morning routines and then meet up in the kitchen before the kids go off to school (who is driving them today?) and my husband and I go to work. Once again, we Talk Day, restating what was established the night before.

This system is extremely helpful, somewhat annoying, and definitely funny. It has become our own quirky family ritual. I'm not sure whether it keeps me structured and sane or structured and frazzled. Probably both.

I love to go to the movies. I love the experience. It's like an event that is your own. The darkness, your attention, the solitude (even when you are with someone). Plus, now that every theater has the reclining chairs, there's nothing better! It actually brings me joy. Every time I go to the movies with my husband and/or kids, as soon as we sit down and are situated with our snacks—large popcorn, peanut M&Ms, possibly Twizzlers and Junior Mints, and, of course, because I am dedicated to healthful eating, a large Coke Zero—I turn to each of them, squeeze their legs, and say, "This is so fun!" Just pure, innocent, true fun.

I even have this same experience when I go to the movies alone. I literally tell myself how much fun I am having—and I mean it.

There are some times, however, when, just before I go into the theater, I'm a mess. It's because I sometimes go to the movies to relieve stress. There are definitely times at the office where things are too much. When that happens, I usually try to formulate a plan as to how to solve the problem. But other times, I pull up Fandango and check the movie times.

Happily, there are two movie theaters right near the Premier offices. And they're the good kind of theaters—huge, with reclining seats and enormous sodas. At those times of stress, I really don't care what movie I see. I just need the experience. *The Texas Chainsaw Massacre*, *Cloudy with a Chance of Meatballs*, *The Butler*—they're all good. Whatever it is, I can escape and come out just that little bit happier.

Sometimes the key to balancing the demands of work with the demands of family is to escape from both for a while.

I have been working a lot recently—like, a lot. And not on minor things, either, but on major things that for some miserable reason all seem to be converging at once. This is a primo *My Cousin Vinny* moment, as in, "How much more shit can we pile onto this pile of shit?", or something to that effect.

When this happens, as you can imagine, I become stressed, snippy, impatient, and aloof. Unfortunately, my family sees this. I suppose one solution would be to just sleep in the office until the toughest times are past. It is doable: My office does have a couch, and the building does have a shower. It's probably not very realistic, however.

A better approach might be to meditate, "leave it at the office," and be sunshine and unicorns when I rejoin the family circle. I haven't quite gotten there yet. So my flawed self has been revealing itself in full glory as of late.

Aware of my behavior, and drowning in guilt, I decided to have a conversation with Maccabi about how I am doing as a mother. We do have open and honest conversations like this, and I am very thankful for them. Without hesitation, my son confirmed that my stress level was too high, that I was working too much, and that I was too "on" him. (Actually, I disagree with this last part. As I say to him, his friends, the ones whose parents aren't "on them"—well, those parents simply don't love their kids. I don't think he buys this yet.)

On balance, however, I accepted Maccabi's insights. We discussed them and came up with a plan: I will try to decompress, and only do work at home when he is doing homework. The "on him" part will essentially have to stay. If he keeps making good grades, maybe I will back off a bit. (Who am I kidding!)

This agreement was a fine accomplishment for the two of us and our relationship. But I clearly wasn't in peak form that night. Because I pressed on, asking him how would he rate me as a mother, using a scale of one to five.

Without a thought, Maccabi said, "a three." That quickly followed with his pointing to his father and saying, "He gets a four."

My immediate, loud, and flabbergasted reaction was, "What, a fucking three, are you serious! And he gets a four! I'm the one who has always been around, especially when you were young and I was doing all of the heavy lifting, and now, your father comes home for dinner for a few weeks, and he gets a four!" All of this, of course, amidst hysterical laughter from the whole family.

It was a fun moment. But I was actually very upset. *I'm not doing a good enough job!* I said to myself. As I was outwardly laughing, I was inwardly tearing out my organs.

Some words from seventeen-year-old Ruby helped. "Momma," she asked, "why are you so insecure?" A bit of a silver lining, I guess.

QUOTE UNQUOTE

They say you should never talk about politics and religion. Well, this story has both. It was a Friday night, and my family and some guests were having Shabbos dinner. Friday nights are an important time for us to spend solid, uninterrupted, and fun time together.

This particular Friday dinner was just a few weeks before the 2020 election, and the topic of Donald Trump came up—a polarizing figure, to say the least. Someone in the group declared herself a Trump supporter, which was met with a lot of consternation. To defend her candidate, she asked, "Have you ever met someone so powerful that has such an amazing relationship with their kids?"

To which my kids immediately replied, "Our mom."

Chapter 12

"You Can't Be Serious!"

Relationships are at the core of every business. Inspiring your team members to work hard, to pay attention to detail, and to let their creative juices flow; turning prospects into customers; keeping people calm in a crisis; getting people to believe they *can* be the best—you can't do any of these things unless you have a good feeling for people and how they operate, as well as a strong sense of self and a healthy dose of emotional intelligence.

You don't learn this stuff in business school. You either got it or you don't. And if you got it, you gotsta trust it. Which I do.

The tricky part is that not all people are logical and reasonable. In fact, many of them are ruled by emotions. And sometimes the emotional side of relationships makes doing business almost impossible. This can lead to challenges on a big scale—challenges that only the CEO can manage.

One of the ways I've gotten better at managing the emotional side of business is by learning how and when to allow my own emotions to show.

You remember Tom Hanks as the manager Jimmy Dugan in *A League of Their Own*. When right fielder Evelyn Gardner (played by Bitty Schram) commits a boneheaded play, he reams her out in front of her teammates, reducing her to tears. Which leads to Tom's memorable line: "Are you crying? Are you crying? . . . There's no crying in baseball!"

That used to be my motto: There's just no crying—not in baseball, and certainly not in business.

But I've come to accept the fact that, sometimes, you just have to cry. (Thanks for this insight to my wonderful therapist and my forum mates in the Young Presidents' Organization, all of whom have leant me their supportive shoulders on plenty of occasions over the years.)

Every November, a huge, important dental convention is held in New York City, starting (believe it or not) on the Sunday of Thanksgiving weekend. (Our industry also holds a huge convention in balmy, tropical Chicago every February. We really know how to schedule them, don't we?)

Of course, these gatherings are vital venues for close conversations with many of my important connections in the business. I always attend them along with a group of colleagues from various departments of our company.

One year, the New York convention was especially busy for me, with back-to-back-to-back meetings from early in the morning into the night. I normally thrive on this. I like to be busy; I like to pack my time; and I find it fun and exciting to tell people how amazing Premier is. I don't feel overly tired or hungry until I get back to my hotel room at night, and then I really collapse.

This particular year, however, the convention dates coincided with a time when there were *tons* of important, impactful, and strategic things going on both at Premier and in the industry. So, in retrospect, I was feeling pretty stressed as I worked my way through my day of meetings. But I felt good about the meetings until one particular conversation with an important customer late in the afternoon.

The discussion started okay, although the customer made a point of sharing with me the fact that his company was having serious problems in the marketplace. In fact, they were so squeezed by the competition that they'd felt forced to reduce their prices to the point where they were actually losing money on some of their (and our) most popular products. This naturally led to a discussion of pricing, margins, and acquisition costs—all normal things to discuss at a business meeting, and topics I understood intuitively from my years in the business.

Which made it all the more shocking when he said something to me I'd never heard or imagined before. "Under the circumstances," he said, "I'm sure you understand that you need to give back to us by lowering your prices, so we can make back the deficit we've been experiencing." The customer said this as if it was the most natural thing in the world—regardless of the fact that it was simply absurd.

One of my favorite sayings of late is "this sounds like a *you* problem, not a *me* problem." Given the fact that our two companies—and he and I personally—have been doing business together for years under the fairest pricing practices, this was definitely not a *me* problem.

So I was totally taken aback by his request. The response inside my brain was something like, *What?! Are you fucking kidding me? That would amount to hundreds of thousands of dollars a year for nothing, and negative value to Premier. This is neither sustainable nor acceptable.*

Of course, I kept my control. While I thought this on the inside, on the outside, I continued the discussion with pleasantries and reasonable-sounding observations. I'm sure I looked and sounded like my usual confident, upbeat self. I planned on maintaining this facade until I got to my hotel room that night. I understood that Premier was facing a major business problem. But at that moment, I couldn't allow the other members of my team to know about it. I needed to present them with a solution, not just a problem. I am the CEO—that's my job. So I headed off to my next meeting, internally in a state of shock, insecurity, and disbelief, yet looking like my normal badass self on the outside.

As I was maneuvering my way up the crowded aisle of the Javits Center, I spotted one of my closest friends in the industry heading my way—someone I'd known for over fifteen years. I went up to him with the intention of giving him a drive-by greeting and hug. But the minute I wrapped my arms around him, I started to cry.

My friend panicked. Bursting into tears in the middle of a dental convention is not normal behavior for anyone, and especially not for me. I could only imagine what he was wondering: Had I just gotten horrible news about a fatal medical condition? Or had my favorite reality TV show just been cancelled?

"I'm fine," I reassured him. "Just a little rattled. We can talk about it later. But right now, I don't want anyone else to see me like this!"

I took a moment to wipe my face and compose myself. I gave my friend another hug, and I thanked him for being so amazing, being exactly where I needed him to be, and being ready to support me through a moment I totally had not expected.

I wore my game face for the rest of the day's meetings, and finally headed back to my hotel room, where I gave myself permission to cry some more—while crafting possible solutions on my 8.5" x 11" writing pad.

Yes, you're human, and sometimes you have to let it out. But if you manage it appropriately, you can do it in a way that doesn't dent your image as a leader.

As the story about my convention meeting illustrates, when issues of money arise in connection with an important business relationship—one that has been meaningful to both partners for many years—things can get very emotional, very quickly.

A few years ago, a conflict arose between Premier and one of our business partners. The precise cause isn't important. All you need to understand is that it was a technical matter that made doing business difficult for Premier—until the cause was identified and fixed. Business as usual resumed. Or so I thought. But recently, when I invited this partner to collaborate on a project with us, the executive I spoke with—someone I'd known and worked with for years—seemed hesitant. I asked why, and he said it was because of the "issues" we'd had *over three years earlier*.

I was absolutely floored. *Are we five years old here? Get over it! We have businesses to run.*

Out loud, I said, "You can't be serious!"

"Well, it will take us a while to get over it," the executive said.

"How long will that be?" I asked

"We don't know," he said.

"Well, tell me when it's over," I said, and hung up.

I'm still waiting.

Thankfully, most of the people we do business with aren't such delicate flowers. I usually find that, through patient cultivation combined with the basics—hard work and tenacity—I can maintain solid, mutually beneficial relationships with our important suppliers and customers. In some cases, I've even been able to turn dicey partnerships into much stronger, more sustainable ones.

I try to review vendor contracts annually. It's a discipline, but one that I find valuable and grounding. We had a partner relationship that was governed by an outdated document. I thought it best to revisit if possible.

My father had a different take—he thought it best to let sleeping dogs lie. But my management team shared my view that this was an important issue. I had to readdress this, or at least try.

I got in touch with an executive at the partner company. After a get-to-know-one-another meeting, I asked whether she would be willing to reconsider our contract, and she agreed to open the discussion. Excellent—but just a first step.

Many negotiations followed. Every step along the way was delicate, calling for thoughtful calculations and clear, forthright conversations. Eventually, we hammered out a new arrangement. A formal document blessed by the lawyers was drawn up, and both parties agreed to sign it. But then a long period of silence followed.

Days passed. I began to resign myself to the idea that I'd failed—and to the fact that, if we didn't receive a signed contract after one more day, I would have to look at other possibilities.

All of this was happening while I was on vacation with my family in London. The next day, while having a snack of hot chocolate and scones with my daughter at Le Pain Quotidien, I checked my email. Yes, checking email during family time is a bad habit that I am working to break. But in this case, I'm glad I did it. I saw the email address of our partner. I immediately opened it and clicked on the attachment. She'd sent the signed contract!

I actually started crying, right there in the middle of the café with my daughter. This time, the tears were tears of emotional release. Reams of work had finally yielded the result I wanted. I was proud of myself. It's an emotion that I rarely feel and that I express even less often.

Back in our offices, my management team was thrilled (and, to be honest, I think a bit surprised) when I unveiled the improvement at our next meeting. Unfortunately, my father's immediate reaction was to ask, "How much did this cost us in legal fees?"

I ignored the question. I knew that nailing down that contract had further solidified me as a leader, a force, and a defender of Premier—as well as a businessperson who knows how to ride the emotional ups and downs of business until I achieve the results I need.

As for my father's less-than-supportive comment: I am learning not to let things like this bother me. He means well.

One thing that helps is the growing recognition of my accomplishments by my peers in the dental industry. An indication of this: In recent years, the industry has experienced a lot of consolidations. Distributors have been buying their competitors; larger manufacturers are buying smaller ones. In this environment, Premier has become a hot commodity.

As a result, the highest executives at a financial institution asked to meet with me. The upshot was that they said they wanted to buy Premier—but only if I remained in leadership and if my father was not part of the picture.

(Whoa. *Brutal.*)

For the record, we turned down the offer—not part of Premier's plans—but it's nice to be wanted. And it's even nicer when the people who want you are particularly appreciative of what you as an individual have contributed to the business. Maybe I shouldn't care about what other people think about me—and a lot of the time, I don't. But I'm human, and being seen as a real leader by people I respect is one of those things that helps to make all the hard work and craziness feel worthwhile.

QUOTE UNQUOTE

"Too late—you're already in the ring!" In business, you *will* get sued. You can operate with the highest levels of integrity, with the strongest moral compass—it doesn't matter. At some point, someone will have a problem with you that they believe warrants legal action.

And so, at one point, that is where we found ourselves at Premier—being sued by a very long-standing and trusted partner. Not ideal, but, as I have said before, business is business.

The other truth about being sued is that no one likes it. Who would? It is disruptive, expensive, draining, and uncertain. And perhaps the person that likes being sued the least on the planet is my father. In general, my father is very loving and inclusive, and he values business partnerships. As I've mentioned, he is also completely nonconfrontational, and you don't get much more confrontational than a lawsuit.

So my father desperately wanted this suit to *not* be happening. But there was nothing we could do about that. So you corral your most powerful lawyers, you prepare, you strategize, and, when you must, you fight.

This suit had been going on for a while, and I was in New York City to meet with our attorneys. I was in the cab on the way to their offices, on the phone with my father, and he was trying to dissuade me from taking this further.

I was furious. This was not up to me, and it was not my doing—they'd come for us, and we were defending ourselves. I was making my position very clearly, loudly, and angrily known while in the back of the taxi.

Finally, my father said to me, "I don't want to fight."

My response: "Too late—you're already in the ring!" I hung up, exasperated, and the cab pulled up to the lawyers' offices.

As I was getting out of the taxi, the driver said to me, "You're right! You keep going. Don't let them stop you."

At least *someone* got it!

Long story short: We won the suit, and are still close with these partners today.

Chapter 13

Singing My Way to Success

Being a successful business leader isn't all about mental and emotional toughness—essential as those are. It's also about engaging with people—inspiring them, uplifting them, and helping them to feel that being part of your team is the most creative, productive, and enjoyable thing they can do with their careers.

And that's where one of my most ridiculous secret talents comes into play. It's the talent that has probably disqualified me from doing incredible things: earning a PhD in neuroscience, becoming an expert in constitutional law, not getting lost every time I get in my car. My brain capacity has been used up on the ability to write song lyrics. Not brilliant song lyrics on a par with, say, "Stairway to Heaven," "The Obvious Child," or "Gold Digger," but lyrics to superimpose onto existing popular songs to relay a fun or quirky message. The kinds of lyrics that emerge when I decide I need to write a ditty for my grandmother's birthday, so I'll steal the tune to "Hollaback Girl."

That, ladies and gentlemen, is my gift.

It started out as something fun that we would do as a family: a, yes, birthday song for my grandmother, a fun message for my husband, or something cute for the kids. I remember one night during a large family vacation (siblings, aunt, and cousin included), we put together an extended version of "Macarena" for our grandmother Malvina. My favorite verse recounted a family tale from World War II. While my grandfather was serving in Europe, my grandmother gave birth to her first child (my father). So there she was, a young, first-time mother alone in New York City—a stressful time, to say the least. One day, feeling overwhelmed, she knocked on her neighbor's apartment door, said, "Take my baby," and handed him over. (Of course, she later took the baby back, and survived to become the most powerful, wise, influential, and beautiful woman I know.)

The songwriters who created the original "Macarena" probably never thought their tune would be used with a story like this.

I have taken this absurd and useless skill and transferred it to business settings. Most years, Premier is invited to participate in dealer trade shows, which are events set up like any industry convention. There are hundreds of attendees, booths hosted by dozens of companies, and keynote speeches by industry leaders. These events give us a chance to interact with our distribution partners and their sales reps, teaching them about Premier's products. The result is essentially two to three straight days of five-minute presentations to groups of sales reps who become increasingly dazed, exhausted, and bored.

So how do we break through and make these interactions fun? That's right: comical lyrics about Premier's dental products set to the tunes of top twenty hits. For example, one of my favorites is "My Life Is Great with Premier," set to the tune of Kelly Clarkson's "My Life Would Suck Without You." We set up our booth with bales of hay, a stage, and a microphone (unlike practically every other booth, which featured a table displaying dental instruments, cements, and other relevant but numbingly familiar stuff).

When the first round of reps started streaming onto the show floor, they took a look at us and thought they had hit the wrong hotel ballroom. But then we introduced ourselves and started to sing. They were amazed, then broke into hysterical laughter. We had taken a mundane experience and turned it into a memorable and fun event.

Not to brag, but I am able to create these masterpieces in mere minutes. Case in point: One year, the theme for one of these trade shows was "Made in the USA." Perfect! Premier would, of course, go with a Bruce Springsteen theme, and I wrote a corresponding song. But just hours before everything was due to be submitted, I found out that one of our competitors was also doing a presentation with a Bruce theme. We certainly could not run the risk of appearing to be mere copycats. What to do?

I quickly went online to search for songs with America in their name. What popped out was "American Woman" by the unmatched Lenny Kravitz. That was all I needed. Fifteen minutes later, "American Sales Reps" was born. Unless you were in the dental supply business, you never had the chance to enjoy it, but take it from me—it was a huge hit on the trade show floor.

Next up was another national sales meeting, hosted by a major player in the dental industry that was also one of our customers. The challenge was to produce a thirty-to-forty-five-second video recorded by a representative of each company highlighting that company's unique characteristics. I was nominated by our team to be the spokesperson. No boring talking head speech from me—I would leave that for the cookie-cutter CEOs. My head went straight to Will Smith: "In West Philadelphia born and raised / in dental is where I spend most of my days . . ."

Goofy and ridiculous? Of course. Serious and dignified, as

befits the leader of an important company in an industry dealing with urgent issues of health care? Definitely not. But out of the hundreds of professionals who attend the conferences that Premier participates in, almost none will remember what our industry peers have to say—but they all remember the CEO of Premier, happily making a fool of herself with a song about what makes her company unique.

Of course, any special talent can become routine and boring if it's trotted out on every occasion. So I've had to come up with other ways of making Premier's participation in industry events fun and memorable, beyond catchy songs.

One of our industry's long-standing traditions started some thirty plus years ago. More than a business event, it was an annual luncheon at the meeting of the Dental Manufacturers of America (DMA). (You know the sort of meeting—held at a resort, featuring lots of speakers, lots of networking, and lots of ideas.) The luncheon was a fun event at which personal friendships would be renewed along with useful business connections.

Let me digress for a moment to explain something about the social realities of our business. Initially, when trade associations first came to our industry, there were actually two trade organizations. One was the American Dental Trade Association (ADTA), made up mostly of dental distributors, which, at the time of its founding, did not allow Jewish people to participate. Yes, sad to say, what some refer to as "genteel anti-Semitism" was once a real thing in American businesses. In 1932, responding to this distressing phenomenon, my grandfather and others created the DMA, made up mostly of companies that manufactured dental products and supplies, and they obviously accepted Jews. I grew up going to the DMA events, and I loved them! I got to go to swank hotels (my grandmother used to say, "We're fancy ladies!"), go swimming, buy bubblegum-flavored lip gloss from the gift shops, and watch TV in our room while my grandfather and father attended their meetings.

Thankfully, over time, the world became more accepting. The ADTA began accepting Jews. Decades later, in 2004, it merged with the DMA, forming the Dental Trade Alliance (DTA). And our annual two-family luncheon event continued, now a feature of the DTA meetings. As our respective companies grew, those in attendance included not just the biological families, but the business families as well. From your own business experience, you may know how those lunches go, too: a light meal with fun conversation and some talk about business trends and ideas.

As I got older and became part of the business, I realized two things. First, we should be having these lunches with more of our customers. Events like this represent a great opportunity to deepen the personal and business connections with people who matter to us, and we should be making the most of them.

Second, why not make our lunches into something much bigger and more unusual than a mere lunch? And so, the fun, creativity, and planning kicked in.

Creating an exciting and successful event for attendees at a DTA meeting is more complicated than you might think. It starts with careful analysis of the schedule for the upcoming DTA gathering. There is usually at least one afternoon free, one late afternoon free, and one dinner held as an optional industry event. I try to schedule an event during one of these free periods with each of our major customers. It's a tricky challenge. One group is comprised of big golfers, so the free afternoon can't be with them—they will be golfing. One team likes to do the optional dinner event, so that slot has to go to someone else. Eventually, we figure out whom we can host during each of the available windows.

Then the real brainstorming begins. What can we do that is more than just a meal—something unexpected, laughter-producing, unforgettable, even epic?

Over the years, we've come up with a variety of ideas. Four events in particular really stand out for me.

The first was the Beach Olympics. All the attendees—spouses and families included—were divided up into teams and invited to participate in competitive events like those you might find at a summer camp. We had the bucket challenge: who could fill up their buckets with the most ocean water, despite the fact that the buckets had holes at the bottom? Then there was the water balloon toss, sand castle construction, and other wacky sports. The basic idea was to give a bunch of adults an excuse to act like idiots on the beach, getting sweaty, covered in sand, and a chance to be competitive.

Sadly, my team lost that year. (Yes, I have been known to get seriously competitive, even when the competition is fundamentally crazy and meaningless.)

A second popular event was our *Iron Chef*-style competition. We turned a hotel ballroom into our version of the Kitchen Stadium. Each team of cooks was given its own mini-kitchen—complete with stove burners, blenders, and woks—along with basic foodstuff and a "secret ingredient" to use in preparing a dish (in this competition, it was squash). Now, I can't cook for shit—but Peter on my team could! My contribution was out-of-the-box thinking. I reasoned that no one else would probably be making a squash dessert, so we grilled squash and served it with maple syrup and cinnamon.

I thought this innovative approach would win us the championship, but we came in second. Not too bad.

The third event was a mixology competition—essentially *Iron Chef* but with alcohol. You can't get much better than that! I discovered that Dan on my team had once been a bartender. Woo-hoo! He knew what flavors went with what, what garnishes to choose, what glasses to use, even what type of ice to add. There were two challenges set up. In the first, each team had to make the same drink; in the second, each team had to concoct their own drink. We went with something tropical and minty, kind of mojito-esque.

Once more, my team was not a winner, but we came in second (again), and the whole event was totally hilarious.

The last event was a scavenger hunt. We had clues to follow that led each team all over the property, traveling in a golf cart provided for the purpose. At each stop, we had an activity to complete, and we needed to take pictures to prove that we had completed every task. They ranged from proving we'd made it to different rooftops to finding a dog statue on the far side of the resort. My team went a step further: We found a couple of guests with a real dog and took a picture of them in front of the dog statue! We got no extra points for our creativity, however.

My team did devise one strategy that we thought was pure genius: We commandeered a groundsman who worked at the resort! He cruised around with us and helped us decode all of the clues. How could we not win?!

Well, once again, we didn't win. But we had a ridiculously fun time.

Clearly, I am not the best at crazy, campy games. (No, I am not bitter. At least, not very.) But I am great at coming up with games and creating an unusual and unforgettable experience for all involved. Maybe next year will be my turn on the winners' podium. After all, I do organize these things—there must be some way to guarantee a victory!

As you can see, I have a talent for helping people to bond through activities that are silly and fun. But business isn't always about being frivolous. When times are tough, the best way to connect with people may be to be honest and authentic—to share your struggles with others who are affected by them.

At the end of each year, we hold an internal Premier town hall where I speak about the business and we acknowledge employees with many years of service. When the town hall is held in conjunction with our holiday party, we throw in a ping-pong tournament or a game of Premier Family Feud. We believe in fun!

But one year had been a particularly tough one for Premier. The industry was down, our regulatory costs were up, we couldn't sell some of our major products into Europe, and everyone was working very hard to combat these things.

As I thought about what I was going to say at that year's town hall, I debated about how forthcoming I should be. Should I spin everything positively, solely highlighting the achievements that we did have, or should I be more transparent and balanced?

I decided that being honest about our circumstances would humanize me, showing my vulnerabilities as a person and a leader. It would let our team know that I understood how rough the year had been for them, and that it had been rough for me, too.

So what should I say; how should I start? As so often happens, my mind gravitated to TV shows and movies. In this case, I remembered a scene from my favorite movie, *My Cousin Vinny*. Mona

Lisa Vito (played by Marisa Tomei in an Oscar-winning performance) has been stiffed by J.T. (Chris Ellis), a local whom she beat in a game of pool. Mona Lisa and Vinny (Joe Pesci) head over to the bar where the pool game had taken place to find J.T. and collect the money he owes her.

They find J.T. and Vinny demands the money. (Note that J.T. towers over Vinny by about ten inches and has a good seventy-five pounds of extra muscle, too.) The following dialogue ensues:

J.T.: How 'bout if I just kick your ass?

Vinny: Oh, a counteroffer. That's what we lawyers—I'm a lawyer—we lawyers call that a counteroffer. This is a tough decision you give me here. Get my ass kicked or collect $200. Hm. Let me think . . . I could use a good ass-kickin', I'll be very honest with you . . . hm . . . nah, I think I'll just go with the two hundred.

J.T.: Over my dead body.

Vinny: You like to renegotiate as you go along, huh? Okay then, here's *my* counteroffer . . . Do I have to kill you? What if I was just to kick the ever-loving shit out of you?

J.T.: In your dreams.

Vinny: Oh, no, no, no . . . in reality.

That was it! That was how I would start my town hall—by showing this clip about getting your ass kicked. It would be funny, engaging, and create the mood I sought without being too in your face.

It worked (although my father told me, after my speech, that he'd thought I was "sending the wrong message"). The clip set the tone for the day and for the upcoming year. It brought levity and humor to what otherwise might have been a damp review of a difficult twelve months.

Most important, it reinforced the feeling that anything is possible. After all, in the movie, Vinny ends up winning the fight with J.T. and collecting Mona Lisa's money—despite the fact that Vinny should never have been able to beat him. I believed that Premier, too, could rise above its underdog status and come out on top in the months to come. Which is exactly what happened—the message I chose to send was the right one.

The importance of sending clear, compelling messages is something I've thought a lot about since my early days at CNN and AIPAC. The stories in this chapter aren't just about having fun—although I definitely believe we could all use more fun in business. They're about making powerful connections with people as a way of strengthening our family business both internally and externally.

In real estate, there's something called staging—creating a context for the property you are selling that will show it to its best advantage. I apply this same thinking to meetings, conferences, training programs, and any other event where people gather and spend time together. I ask: What message are we trying to convey? What results are we trying to achieve? And what kind of narrative will help our message look the best and make it easy for people to want to live in it and make it their own?

That's the purpose behind all my seemingly goofy ideas, from movie clips to party games to comical songs. They're all about helping people become intrigued, then engaged, then invested in Premier—creating a scenario that leaves everybody laughing . . . and winning.

Chapter 14

Holy Fucking Shit

In March 2020 COVID-19 hit. It was the ultimate time for a leader to lead.

The arrival of the COVID-19 pandemic had an almost immediate impact on our business. At first, it seemed as though the devastation would be serious but manageable. I sent out video messages to our team, to the dentists, and to the industry about how Premier had weathered many other crises. After all, our company was over a century old. We'd survived the 1918 influenza epidemic, the Great Depression, and the so-called Great Recession of 2008. I made it very clear that, just as we had during those hard times, Premier would persevere and emerge stronger.

I actually even believed that.

For a while, sales were definitely slowing, but at a rate we could handle. As I've explained, we live by my grandfather's adage, "The dollar is round," which means that we are fiscally conservative and operate with barely any debt. Having identified "operational excellence" as one of our strategic goals well before the pandemic hit, we had already started looking closely at our organization and examining how best to maximize both its capabilities and value. What we learned, placed in the context of the early days of the pandemic, was actually exciting and reassuring. While Premier wasn't as efficient as it could be, the COVID-19 crisis was forcing us to implement changes that should have probably been made earlier.

The last conversation among my leadership team to finalize our plans for the necessary restructuring and new processes lasted six hours—six hours on the phone, of course, as everyone had to stay at home. But as that marathon meeting ended, I was filled with a sense of calm and confidence.

Then March 16th happened.

On that day, the American Dental Association mandated that all dental offices close except for emergency procedures. Emergency procedures account for roughly 25 percent of what is done in the typical dental office. So right off the bat, our sales were essentially down by 75 percent. But many of our products didn't even apply to the 25 percent of business that remained. You do the math.

My reaction was simple and immediate: *Holy shit, what do I do?*

I had a call with my good friend and mentor, Professor Boris Groysberg of Harvard Business School (HBS). I'd come to know him through a joint program between the Young Presidents' Organization and HBS—a kind of mini-business school. Dr. Groysberg was the most amazing of the professors—in fact, within a minute of the start of his lecture, I knew that he was special.

I ended up attending the HBS program for several years, and, after the second year, I mustered the courage to ask if Dr. Groysberg would be willing to work with Premier. Knowing that he works with mega-important companies, I assumed the answer would be an immediate "No." But he agreed, and that is when our friendship, and his mentorship of me, began.

So now I asked Dr. Groysberg for his help in preparing for the possibility that the pandemic might turn out to be more serious and more long-lasting than we'd feared—that perhaps it could devastate both the national economy and the dental industry in particular for many months to come. How could Premier survive such an assault?

He advised me to make a list of the twenty people that would be my core team if the worst should happen. I did that. Then I got started on scenario planning, creating spreadsheets that reflected three possible financial pathways that the market might take—one the best, one the worst, and one in the middle that I considered realistic.

Looking at those spreadsheets for the first time is when the reality of COVID-19 actually set in for me. Once I saw what those scenarios actually looked like, I was suffocated by darkness. I realized that the dire situation I'd discussed with Dr. Groysberg was actually on our doorstep.

I made the decision to furlough more than 80 percent of our employees. This was the absolute worst decision that I'd ever had to make. It was also undeniably the right decision. But even though I knew this to be the case, it decimated me.

From the outset of the pandemic, I did not include my father in most of the decision-making process or in my discussions with key advisors and Premier's leaders. Based on the way our business was structured when I became CEO, the control was mine and I chose to exercise it. Of course, I would speak with my father and seek his guidance about significant decisions. But the truth is that we usually disagree about how to handle many things related to Premier. As the pandemic swept our country and the world, I was under plenty of stress (like most other leaders in every sector). I did not need to compound it with arguments that I knew would be pointless and unhelpful.

Of course, my father was well aware of the dire straits that

Premier was in—like the members of our leadership team and others close to the business, he receives a daily sales spreadsheet by email. Naturally, he was concerned about the future of the business. Periodically, he would call me to ask what I was working on and to get an update on the situation. I kept my answers brief, simply explaining to him the gravity of the situation and the complexity of the decisions that I was making.

One of my father's most consistent and enviable qualities is that he is an eternal optimist. He sees the bright side of every situation and shares this vision with everyone he speaks to. This is often needed—it can be a helpful way to boost the morale of team members when they are uncertain about the future.

Now, during the downward spiral of COVID-19, I found my father's optimism unbearable. Sometimes, after getting a daily sales report that showed a slight uptick in our revenue numbers, he would call me to say, "We had a pretty good day today!"

The problem was that that "pretty good day" reflected a 90 percent drop from our usual daily sales. As the leader who had to manage the painful reality this represented, I just couldn't deal with my father's rosy interpretations.

When I told my father about the need to furlough almost all of our employees, he got very upset. His anger was not directed toward me. He naturally felt a very deep connection to all of our people, as did I, and he did not want this to be the reality, nor did I. But it was the reality—and he took out his frustration on me.

Of course, I tried to help my father understand the decision. I showed him the numbers, explained the market dynamics, and told him that I wasn't alone in my thinking. "Our advisory board agrees with me," I said. "There's really no other choice if we want to stay in business."

That angered him even more. "They don't run the business, we do!" he declared.

"*I* run the business," I reminded him, "and this is what has to be done."

He wasn't satisfied. "If you think the advisory board knows what they are doing," he said, "I want to hear from them myself." He announced his intention to place calls to two of the board members he felt closest to.

I actually wanted to facilitate that, so I got in touch with all of the board members and set up a call, including my father, for that very night—just two days before the furlough plan would be announced.

The call was unendurable. One by one, the members of the board explained to my father why this is what had to be done. He argued with them, basically refusing to recognize the validity of the facts presented to him. The alternative suggestions he offered were hopelessly inadequate—basically using tweezers to remove a tree branch.

After an hour of this, I lost it. My voice raised, I summed up the reality of the situation one more time. "This is *not* a situation in which a surgical approach will work. I wish it was. But we have to take big steps, and we have to take them immediately. That's the only hope we have of preserving Premier and the amazing company that you, your father, and your grandfather built." I was getting increasingly upset, because my father seemed unable to comprehend that I was doing all this to protect him and his legacy.

Still, he argued back. We went around in circles for a few more minutes. Finally, I found myself yelling and crying. "This is the most difficult decision I've ever had to make. It'll probably be the most difficult decision I'll *ever* have to make. Why are you making it worse? This is not what my father should be doing!"

This seemed to get through to him. "No one wanted this to happen," he said. "It's a situation not of our making and not within our control."

"No shit, Dad," I said. "But what *is* within our control is how we deal with it. And this is how I will deal with it." The discussion was over.

I spent the next two days crafting the statements I would use to announce the furloughs, crying, and dry heaving.

There would be three Zoom calls. The first call would be for a handful of people in the company who would be staying on full-time—the core group that I planned to build a new Premier around when the disaster receded. The second call would be for the other few people who would be staying on part-time. The third call would be for the remaining majority of our people, all of whom would be furloughed for at least six months.

Each call would start with an overview of what the dental industry was facing due to COVID-19 and how it was directly impacting Premier. I would then explain that, because of the devastating nature of this situation, we needed to make some very significant and difficult changes, including furloughing the majority of our employees. In this respect, all three calls were the same—but obviously the third call would be by far the most painful, for me and especially for the people on the receiving end of the message.

I got through the first two calls okay, although it was very hard for me to speak—I was choking back tears. The team members I was speaking to were learning that their colleagues and friends were about to lose their livelihoods, and that the Premier they'd come to know and love would no longer exist, at least for a while. Horrible news to listen to. Still, the people on the first two calls were retaining their jobs in at least some capacity, which meant they were comparatively lucky, so conveying the news to them wasn't nearly as difficult as I knew the third call would be.

Before I made that call, I phoned Arlo, our head of human resources and one of my best friends. There's a common belief that it's a mistake to work with a friend. All I can say is, "Thank G-d for Arlo." If there was ever a time when I needed a friend who was also a colleague, this was it.

So I called Arlo after finishing the second call to get her feedback and her advice about the third, hardest call.

"How did I do?" I asked her. "Was everything okay?"

"Everything was fine, Jule," she said. But Arlo and I are so close that I could tell from her voice that something was up.

"Oh shit," I said, "did I say something that I shouldn't have? Was my delivery off? Just tell me so I can adjust for the next call."

"No, nothing like that," Arlo said. "But you know, your father was here in the office, and he asked if he could watch the Zoom call with me." I'd deliberately refrained from telling my father the time of the call because I didn't have the emotional strength to deal with his reactions, my reactions, and the reality of the situation. But he'd somehow found out about it and done this end run on my plan.

Well, I was going to have to hear about it sooner or later. "Okay, what did he have to say?"

"He told me to tell you that, in the next call, you shouldn't use the word 'devastating.' He said you should say 'difficult' instead."

Needless to say, I didn't take his advice.

I honestly don't remember much about the third call. Somehow I got through it. When I logged off of Zoom, I was feeling shattered. I gave myself time to cry.

Then it was back to work. Premier would never be the same—but I still had a business to run, and there were still employees, customers, suppliers, patients, and other partners depending on us. It was time to get started on the new normal.

As I would on any ordinary work day, I began by opening up my email inbox. I immediately saw that it was filled with messages from the furloughed employees. I tensed up. I could only imagine the subject lines the emails would have—phrases like, "Wrong move," "Big mistake," or "You'll be sorry."

But then I started reading. The emails actually carried titles like, "I'm thinking of you," "XOXO," and "Thank you."

The word *awestruck* barely encapsulates what I felt as I read these messages. Humbled, depressed, uplifted. I had just told these people that they would not be employed for the foreseeable future, that there was no certainty about their return—and *they* were concerned about *me*. What incredible, thoughtful, and genuine people we had in the Premier family.

Going through these emails made me question again the decisions that I had made. The people sending those messages were clearly special individuals. How horrible was I, to be letting them go at this time of economic and social turmoil? But the numbers didn't lie. I had no choice but to make this decision if there was to be any hope that Premier would survive.

I finally realized: I'm not a horrible person. I'm a leader.

But now I really had to lead. Under worse circumstances than I'd ever experienced, worse than any of us had ever imagined.

Yet another spreadsheet. I felt as if I'd pored over hundreds of spreadsheets. Best case, worst case, realistic case. Variations on all three cases—with or without a marketing budget, with or without a manufacturing budget, with or without sales people. And on and on. This was my life for at least eighteen hours a day and for more than two months after the arrival of COVID-19. What a mess.

I know myself and my capabilities pretty well. On a good day, I am fairly analytical. On a day where I am faced with the possibility that our fourth-generation family business, responsible for hundreds of employees and their loved ones, may die a sudden death due to a global pandemic, I am basically psychotic. This was the possibility I had to study and analyze every day, multiple times a day. I used the spreadsheets and the scenarios they embodied to devise our strategy, to organize and lead our remaining team members, and to ground myself in the unfortunate reality that this could be it.

I got everyone to work. The very idea seemed counterintuitive: "Hey, team—our sales are down 90 percent, our industry is completely shut down, so now let's go out there and kill it!"

But this was the only way. People need a sense of guidance, a sense of purpose, a sense of possibility, and a sense of pride, no matter how dire the circumstances they are forced to deal with. And, to be honest, this was all that I knew to do—act.

So I got started. I divided our remaining people into cross-functional teams:

- Sales and marketing
- Development and manufacturing
- Finance, customer experience (CX), information technology (IT), and operations
- Leadership

Then I devised a spreadsheet (yes, another one) that reflected each teams' goals, which team member was responsible for what, and the expected completion date.

The goals were divided into two categories: "Immediate" and "Immediate Lite." There was nothing we were focused on that was anything less than urgent. There would be calls every day with the various teams to ensure that every task on our IIL Matrix was being accomplished. On Mondays, I met with the whole team; on Tuesdays, the leadership team; on Wednesdays, the manufacturing and development team; and on Thursdays, the finance/ops team. Fridays were set aside for follow-up meetings.

These meetings turned into powerful tools for remaking Premier to meet the new demands created by the ultra-harsh business environment. For example, on one of the ops team calls, someone mentioned an order we'd received from Russia and wondered whether or not we could fill it. "What's the issue?" I asked. "Is it our inventory levels? Is it their ability to pay? What is the roadblock?"

"Well," I was told, "the issue is that it usually takes four people to process an order like this due to regulatory needs, shipping, and payment terms. And those people are furloughed at the moment."

I was shocked. Four people to process one order? Even when the world is in a good place, that shouldn't be the case. Now, it was simply not doable.

"Next week," I said, "show me the new system or process where this order can be processed with two people."

They did. And we made similar changes in many other areas of our business—changes we should have made earlier, but which we were now forced to make by the cruel world of COVID-19. We introduced new processes and new forms of efficiency—which in the long run should ultimately generate greater profits.

This is what our business was like for two solid months. There was no upsurge in sales, no movement in the industry, but there was a growing sense of purpose and commitment within our team.

Still, there's no doubt these early months of COVID-19 felt nightmarish. Fear, confusion, uncertainty—these are the emotions our core team was feeling as we turned the page to the future.

As their leader, I began to ask myself: How can I transform these emotions into something positive, even in these extraordinary times? How could I turn this angst into a driver of motivation, energy, perhaps even excitement?

The answer, I realized, was branding.

It may sound flippant considering the circumstances, but branding is exactly what was called for. All of the members of my executive team had previously worked for enormous companies— companies where they were valued and did important work, but were unable to make a personal impact. They'd come to Premier for the opportunity to grow, create, and execute a vision that would truly change the trajectory of an organization and affect an entire industry. I needed to tap into that desire to lead, to produce, and to pioneer.

So that is how I branded that core group of team members: The Premier Pioneers. This was the group that would navigate uncharted territories, implement revolutionary strategies, and develop organization-saving efficiencies in a time of unprecedented pain and uncertainty.

I built this branding, one step at a time, in the days and weeks that followed.

Every email that I sent out began with: "Hello Pioneers!"

Every meeting was entered into calendars with the subject: "Premier Pioneers."

We were now part of a collective movement, a movement for sustenance, change, and growth. A movement for both revival and metamorphosis. And this fact became a galvanizing force. It drove people to work harder than they ever had in their careers. It created a willingness to sacrifice much of their time and part of their salaries. It created a community of purpose.

The Premier Pioneers were not recreating the old Premier. They were bringing into existence Premier 2.0—a company that would be stronger, more dynamic, and more profitable.

As we exchanged hundreds of messages during the spring and summer of 2020, every time there was a positive development, I would sign off with "All right, Premier 2.0!"

Whenever I had discussions with customers, competitors, and industry contacts, I would tell them about Premier 2.0 and the energy that our team was generating around it.

When I communicated by video with our team members on furlough, I talked about how Premier 2.0 would emerge from this crisis.

Premier 2.0 was our mantra.

The most satisfying moments came when I got unsolicited emails from our team members that also said "Go Premier 2.0" or "All right, Pioneers." That told me that our new branding was winning a place in the hearts and minds of our people. It was working the way a great brand should.

As we all learned to live with the extended onslaught of COVID-19, the sense of fun that had always been a crucial element in my leadership style reemerged, perhaps slightly dimmed but still strong. Although there were absolutely times during this period when I had to communicate with my team about the pain and struggle we were all experiencing, I tried to balance that with humor and enjoyment. Against all odds, we needed to experience some sense of normalcy.

I accomplished this in several ways. Every Pioneer meeting began with "The Question of the Day"—essentially icebreakers for the whole team that everyone on the call had to respond to. My favorite question was, "What was your nickname growing up? If you didn't have one, what nickname would you have liked to have had?" Some of the answers were hilarious. One of our people had been a big online poker player, and her nickname was Trixxy (she was very adamant about making sure we understood there were two Xs in Trixxy).

Another thing that I did was create Julie's Hangouts, a series of interviews that I conducted with industry leaders. The interviewees included the chief marketing officer of Henry Schein, the dean of the University of Pennsylvania School of Dental Medicine, the chief dental officer of Colgate, and other luminaries. We talked about the challenges they were facing during COVID-19, how their businesses were operating, and the best practices they'd developed.

I called the last part of the interview "Inside the Actors Studio," stealing a little fun from the show hosted for twenty-two years by the late James Lipton. At the end of each program, Lipton would ask the famous actor who was his guest a series of fun, personal, quirky questions, usually requiring short, simple answers. I did the same.

Of course, one of the questions I had to ask was, "What is your favorite movie?" You can imagine my delight when the dean of Penn Dental Medicine answered, *My Cousin Vinny.*

Even in times of crisis, you gotsta keep it real, you gotsta keep it fun, and you gotsta do it together.

QUOTE UNQUOTE

One night during COVID-19, as I was cleaning the kitchen, I was listening yet again to the original cast album of *Hamilton*. I wasn't listening closely until I heard the members of the company singing, to George Washington, the words "history has its eyes on you."

I stopped what I was doing, wondering about that line. What does it mean? Does it apply to me?

Clearly, I am not George Washington or a person of any particular import, yet those lyrics hit me. Would history be watching me? What would it see? What would it say? I have been leading, but have I been doing it correctly? Have I made the right decisions, have I guided us through crises to success? Does anything I do even matter? Who am I and what have I accomplished?

"History has its eyes on you." What do I want history to see—the reality, the authenticity, or the glossy presentation? Do I want it to see the pain, the self-doubt, the exhaustion, the guilt? Should it see the internal struggle to continue, or should it see a veneer of fortitude, confidence, and joy?

I suppose a person either allows the present to simply happen, or crafts the present to deliver what they want history to see. I am unsure as to which one of those people I am, or which one of those I should be.

As I was about to start rinsing out a pot, the *Hamilton* soundtrack still in the background, King George III launched into his song addressing Americans after the revolution. He sang about how hard it is to lead, and asked whether we have a clue as to what would happen next.

"Holy shit," I thought. "I don't."

Chapter 15

What's Next?

Throughout 2020, as the devastation of COVID-19 continued to take its toll on the world, I began to think about . . . the supply chain.

Yes, I realize how pathetic that may sound. I wasn't thinking about health, safety, or even humanity—I was worried about the shipping and receiving of goods. But as you probably realize, aside from health and safety, the supply chain actually turned out to be one of the most important impacts of the pandemic. As a business leader, I realized that we needed to focus on it before most people were paying attention to it.

My first thought was, *We need to bring in a lot of inventory, especially the stuff we source from China, because who knows what will happen with borders, customs, and so on.* So I quickly called up our head of purchasing and our chief financial officer to say, "Buy! Buy!" like they do on the floor of the stock exchange. I told them, "Look at our current inventory levels, and see if we can increase them by at least 40 percent." Smart move! I was feeling good about myself.

Then I watched CNN some more. I learned that Italy was completely shut down, and the problems were just beginning. That's one of our markets, and it sounded as though demand there was still headed south. Okay, not feeling so great. Another call to purchasing and finance: "Have we already called the suppliers and ordered additional product? If we have, can we call them and reduce the order size? Great."

Now I was feeling good again. We'll have product when others won't, but we won't be overextended. How smart am I?

More CNN. Now I learned that more European countries were shutting down, and that the U.S. itself would be shutting down soon. Not feeling good any more—not at all. Another call to purchasing and finance. "Have we made the calls? Have we reduced the order levels? Okay, now we need to reach out to stop everything. All of our purchasing will stop. We will not be accepting any inventory, even what we ordered from our suppliers last week."

I'd said it—but I had no idea whether it would fly. How often do you turn around and completely cancel an order you've just made? Under most circumstances, this would be considered unprofessional. Would our suppliers stand for it?

Unbelievably—yes.

Why? The age-old reason: relationships. The same business relationships that generations of Premier and my family have nurtured—and that sometimes have felt like heavy weights to be carried around, making our progress more difficult and stressful—are also keys to our ability to survive terrible times.

Premier has been doing business with many of the same companies and their leaders for years, sometimes even decades. We have always been respectful, responsible, and communicative. We know and understand their businesses, their challenges, and their needs. We know our partners, their kids, and their stories. Most important, we always paid in full and on time. So now they were willing to give us room to breathe.

But I needed to have an even more difficult conversation with these same suppliers: "You know those payments that we have always made in full and on time? Well, that won't be continuing for the foreseeable future. Products that we've already bought and received will not be immediately paid for."

FUCK. Will this fly?

Unbelievably—again, yes.

Why? The same reason. Relationships that have been nurtured into true partnerships. I went on to have extensive, open, and authentic conversations with my counterparts at all of our partner companies. Every one recognized the situation we were in together. We worked out payment structures, time frames, and strategies. We came up with a plan that was painful but that was fair to everybody.

When I hung up the phone after the last call, I cried. The emotions that flooded me were ones of appreciation, humility, and relief.

I am so blessed to have a team who for years have cultivated this extraordinary level of trust. With this as a foundation, Premier will survive.

So the big question of the day—how does a family business continue to adapt successfully in a business world where nothing is certain except constant, unpredictable change?—turns out to have a simple, powerful answer: you build on the strengths that got you this far.

Months passed. The COVID-19 pandemic continued to morph. So did its impact on our society and our economy.

Little by little, various business sectors began to come back online. The dental industry began to revive—after all, people can't put off caring for their teeth forever.

We had furloughed more than 80 percent of Premier's employees. Those that we retained—the Premier Pioneers—included some people working part-time. As demand began to grow, we started bringing people back. First, we converted some part-time employees to full-time jobs. Then we started calling up the people we'd furloughed and asking them to return. Gradually, we got to the point where we had a solid number of people on staff, yet still significantly down from where we started.

All of this was very good news. But it didn't mean the challenges of building a new Premier were behind us.

I called a meeting of the Premier Pioneers to examine where we were. Was the business performing in the way that we had anticipated, following our strategy, and seeing return on investment? This meeting was not called during the depths of COVID-19, when our sales were at rock bottom and our profits were virtually nonexistent. It was called in 2021, when our numbers were making their way back up, our profit margins were high, and our production levels were up by a 30 percent increase even with 20 percent fewer people.

So why was I feeling so annoyed?

While all of the good news was true, I knew that it was not due solely to our efforts. Prior to the meeting, I'd started the analysis, essentially focusing on two things. One is what we call our Focus Products. We have thousands of individual products (referred to as stock-keeping units, or SKUs). After all, Premier is "Inspired Solutions for Daily Dentistry," and that (thankfully) requires a lot of stuff. Since it's hard to strategize about thousands of products, for purposes of active sales and marketing we choose six to ten products on which we will concentrate our spending, our sales reps' time and compensation, and our dealer partnerships. These are our Focus Products.

The second area of strategic emphasis is the launch of new products. We had recently launched the X5, a really cool and unique matrix system. (A matrix system is used to isolate the tooth when the doctor is building it up in the process of restoration.) So in advance of our strategy meeting, I investigated the performance of the X5 as well as our Focus Products.

And, as a result, I was less than thrilled.

First, I saw that, in terms of market share, the sales trend for some of our Focus Products were flat. Then I checked the sales of the X5 and found they were lower than we had initially forecast. Why? It appeared that the product had not been launched with the coverage, excitement, and exposure that it needed.

Upset, I decided to delve even deeper, looking closely at sales of our non-Focus Products. After all, our overall revenue numbers were looking pretty good—we must have been doing something right, no?

Actually, yes and no. I discovered that some of our strong sales, like those in the rest of the industry, were due to simple inertia.

One of the most amazing things about Premier is that we have world-leading brands that are number one in their space despite being literally fifty-plus years old. Of course, this validates the brand and emphasizes the strength of Premier. But it can also serve as a crutch. Our numbers, while excellent, were *not* coming primarily from our areas of concentration. We were benefiting (thankfully) from the overall business recovery dentistry had experienced driven by the slow decline in COVID-19 cases.

So the good mood around the offices of Premier, based on the strength of our recent sales figures, was not a concomitant response to the success of our marketing and sales efforts. It was what former chair of the Federal Reserve Alan Greenspan used to call "irrational exuberance"—enthusiasm driven by success that was partly externally driven, and created and fed by others.

And that's why I wasn't thrilled—not just about the underlying problem I'd recognized, but about the fact that I was pretty much the only person in the company looking closely at this.

Wanting the understanding, input, and involvement of the team, I presented my findings to them. Irrational exuberance was replaced by a sober appreciation of reality—and then a commitment to action. The whole team recognized that the market itself was contributing to our success. To remedy this, and to take control of our own future, I asked them to devise an accountability matrix and a strategy to assure that, going forward, we would be focusing on the right things, measuring everything, altering our tactics to address any shortfalls, and creating alignment between our goals and our strategies.

At the next meeting, I did the listening. Our leadership team presented all the elements of the business, how they were working together, how these should be interwoven, reported, and judged. They shared the matrix they'd devised, which combined all of our product categories into one report showing current figures and recent trends for product sales, market share for each product category, percentage of the business represented by each product category, the spend contributed to each product, and the return on investment (ROI) produced by each product.

What an amazing team! I was elated. I was so appreciative of their understanding, diligence, and commitment. This was a tool that can keep us focused, in control, and aware. In the months and years to come, everyone at Premier will be looking at this matrix, executing to it, and adapting when necessary.

The data shown in the matrix helped us understand even more clearly where our sales and profits were really coming from. They generated some powerful conversation around the need for a new business strategy—one that focused on specific products and categories we'd long taken for granted and therefore not prioritized.

"Our business is going to look a lot different," I observed. "Maybe not as sexy. But a lot more profitable."

To which our chief marketing officer, responded, "That's how Warren Buffett sleeps so soundly every night. He owns thousands of shares of Gillette—and he knows that in the morning, hundreds of millions of men will be shaving their beards with those boring razor blades."

Everybody laughed. "That will be our strategy for 2022," I announced. "BLB—Boring like Buffett."

I just hope we'll be a fraction of a fraction as successful.

There are 160,000 dentists in the United States, some 700,000 in the world—not a huge market. By contrast, there are 328 million people in the U.S. and 7 billion people in the world. The great news: they all have teeth. (Well, almost all.) Premier creates products to help keep teeth healthy. So how do we access all those billions of teeth?

Traditionally, we have done so by developing products for dentists to use in their patients' mouths. Unfortunately, many people don't go to the dentist, or don't go as often as they should, thus limiting Premier's reach. That might change slightly with every innovative solution that we bring to the professional marketplace;

whenever we create a product that makes visiting the dentist easier and more comfortable, it hopefully encourages more people to go. But it's doubtful that Premier products can change the behavior of dental patients on a population-wide scale.

The more I thought about Premier 2.0, the more I realized that we needed to think differently. Maybe, I thought, we need a network of dental hygienists who serve as sales people and brand ambassadors, creating additional business for them, their dental offices, and us—almost the way Avon dealers represent and build that company's brand. No one in the dental industry has ever done anything like that.

My team at Premier drew up some plans for a program like this. We looked at the financials and potential business structures, and we concluded it could actually work. But while I was mulling the idea of launching this project, I got to know a new friend and mentor, a true marketing guru. One evening while the two of us were attending a Miami Heat basketball game, I described the concept to him. He liked the idea, but his main reaction was "You need to think bigger."

That was thought-provoking. I wondered, *What does bigger mean for a company like Premier?*

I started to think about our products and their applications. We at Premier have been pioneers in dental health for over a century. Our products have touched hundreds of thousands of lives and improved them. But while most of our products definitely have everyday use applications, they are medical devices and not permitted for sale to the general public. So how can we get bigger than that? In other words, how can Premier break out of the dental office and become a creator of products that ordinary people use in their daily lives to improve their dental health?

I spent time looking at the products we have and trying to figure out which one—or which combination of products—the general public might want to use at home. Eventually, I hit on an idea that I believed could sell as an initial offering—a combination of products that would serve as the flagship of a new Direct-to-Consumer (DTC) company. It would be an electric toothbrush and electric tooth polisher in one—a tool that would not only brush your teeth but polish them using prophy paste the way the hygienist does at your dental visit. The ads practically write themselves: "Leave your bathroom with that great, straight-from-the-dentist feel."

That was the big idea. As for the details, there were plenty of them and they all needed to be worked out correctly. The delivery system needed to be different from any electric toothbrush currently on the market. Developing it would call for a dedicated R&D program. But that was not a problem; you might recall that Premier has its origins as an instrument company (my great-grandfather Julius was a dental instrument sharpener). We would design a two-in-one toothbrush and polisher with brush heads, prophy angle heads, and a sterilizing station for the brush heads. As a valuable accessory, we could reengineer one of our scalers (a specialized plaque removal tool) to be single ended, less sharp, and made of medical grade plastic. All in matte black, of course, for the cool factor.

To go with this delivery system, the at-home customer would need prophy paste. As you now know, our Enamel Pro® is a market leader in professional-grade prophy paste, but it would need be reformulated to include safe and appropriate levels of pumice and fluoride. Another R&D challenge, but also well within our capabilities.

The more I played with this idea, the more I loved it! But would anybody else love it?

Well, Premier has run one survey after another, both by ourselves and with the help of independent marketing agencies, and all of the data suggest that we have a likely success on our hands.

As you can imagine this has all been tremendously exciting for me. And also very stressful. Moving into the DTC marketplace is a huge deviation. Is it too much of a risk? No one can say for sure, but it's something I worry about constantly. I like to be a pioneer, yet I'm also risk-averse. Knowing that I am laying my reputation and that of Premier on the line for a brand-new concept that may or may not work has caused me some sleepless nights.

Luckily, I have some wise outside counselors to turn to. The most helpful has been Professor Groysberg. He has reminded me that the planning and research we've done—the repeated marketplace surveys, the financial analyses, the two years of concept development—have wrung most of the risk out of the equation. Furthermore, we are not betting the farm on this project. If it fails, we will take a financial hit—but it will be far from fatal, and, in the process, we will learn a lot. This is a textbook example of a calculated risk, which is precisely the kind of business-expanding move that a CEO must take.

So the project is moving ahead at full speed. Our team is pumped, the development and design processes are well under way, and our plans for marketing and sales are taking shape. The new DTC company is ready to be launched, marking a new era in the history of our company.

Until recently, however, there was one thing missing from the package: a brand name.

Dreaming up the brand name for an exciting new product is an important step. The perfect brand can help launch a new offering into the stratosphere. A brand that's lame or confusing may not kill the product, but it can hinder it and lengthen the odds against success.

So I jumped into the name-development process with energy and enthusiasm. I thought of it as creative and fun—and it was. Until it became a huge pain in the ass.

It didn't take much research to uncover the fact that practically every logical possibility for a brand name—and most of the illogical possibilities as well—had already been taken, used, or legally protected. Think of all the words you might associate with a two-in-one toothbrush and polisher for use at home—words like "bright," "gleam," "white," "smile," "shine," "sparkle," "glitter" . . . Every one of them, and countless more, is already owned by somebody. We tried using compound words with similar meanings to the words that were taken; those, too, were already legally claimed by a competitor, except for a few possibilities that were ridiculously awkward and clunky.

Someone on the team suggested we begin looking at foreign languages. Clever idea! I threw out some words in Hebrew that I thought sounded cool and had meanings that were appropriate to our product. No one liked them. My husband, who is South African, speaks Afrikaans, so I asked him to translate words like "bright," "smile," and "sparkle" into that language. The results all looked and sounded something like "*vligechampts*"—unpronounceable and impossible to remember for the average American. (My apologies to readers who are dedicated speakers of Afrikaans.) We ruled those out, too. Forays into other languages produced no better solutions.

Time was running short. We needed a brand name for all kinds of reasons: We had to register it legally with the U.S. Patent and Trademark Office, we needed to include it on the product itself, and we needed a logo design to use on packaging, in advertising, and in marketing. Where could we turn?

As often happens when I am in need of business inspiration, I thought of my grandfather. He was born in the United States, but his father's family was from Lithuania. My grandmother, also born in the United States, was very proud of her Hungarian heritage, and would often tell us stories about playing in the woods with Romani people. With these thoughts in mind, I began playing around with the Google Translate app. I switched among English, Hungarian, and Lithuanian and just started putting in words, especially the litany of words like "bright" and "shine" that we'd already been searching through.

Still, nothing useable came up.

I was running out of steam. I typed in what I told myself would be the last word for the night—"glow"—and asked Google to translated it into Hungarian.

Much to my amazement, there before me appeared a gleaming and perfect word: IZZO. Strong, fun, cool.

When I presented it to the Premier team the next day, they loved it. Hopefully the market will, too!

In early 2021, the first vaccines for COVID-19 became more widely available. We all understood that this did not spell the end of the pandemic, but we knew it represented an important turning point in the battle against the disease.

To celebrate, I wanted to do something meaningful for the Premier team that had been in place throughout the entire period of Armageddon. They had worked their asses off, had their salaries cut, neglected their families—and absolutely crushed it. Definitely deserving of recognition for all they'd sacrificed and all they'd achieved.

So I planned an event at The Logan, a hotel in downtown Philadelphia, for them and their spouses. We scheduled a beautiful outdoor dinner with drinks, sparkly lights, and a menu that included amazing spare ribs (or so I was told—I'm not much of a meat eater). It was the first time that we'd all been together in person in over a year, so that in itself made the night very special.

I decided to keep the program simple. I would be the only speaker, and I was determined to say something meaningful and different—not just a generic speech with praise for the work my team members had done. Instead, I chose one word to describe each person in attendance—a character trait, a way of working, the way that I saw them. I paired each word with an appropriate quotation. I prepared a card for each team member, read their personal word and quotation aloud, then handed the card to them. The words I used included "smart," "willing," "sane," "curious," "compassionate," "analytical," and "excited." For one team member, I chose the word "tireless," and I used a quotation from President Franklin D. Roosevelt: "When you reach the end of your rope, tie a knot in it and hold on."

It was a simple presentation. But the effect was emotional and impactful.

The rest of the night was spent mingling, chatting, laughing, and being "normal," for the first time in many months. Toward the end of the night, as people were leaving, my father came up to me.

"Well, I guess I'll be leaving, too."

"I'll walk you out, Abba," I told him.

We'd all been through one of the most stressful periods of our lives—an emotional carpet-bombing that had strained countless relationships, none more than the one I shared with my father, which had already been a difficult one for both of us. Now, at last, I was beginning to feel a bit of hope.

I turned toward my father as we approached the door of the hotel.

"You know, I want to tell you how much I appreciate the trust you've shown in me. And how grateful I am for the opportunity you gave me to lead Premier. I hope you know how much these things mean to me."

My father was silent for a moment. Then he smiled, and, as he opened the door to leave, he gave me the best answer I could have imagined. "Well, Julie," he said, "you are Premier now." That was easily the highlight of the night, and the year.

QUOTE UNQUOTE

"A part of you belongs to Premier." This is another cherished Mortonism. My grandfather liked to speak these words over the office intercom every Friday afternoon and before every work holiday. It was his way of encouraging us to enjoy quality time with family and friends, while not losing sight of the company we are proud to be a part of, and that we represent.

"Corporate culture" wasn't a thing that people talked about much during Grandpa's years at the helm of Premier. But this saying certainly positively solidified how people felt about working at Premier. Morton Charlestein had an instinctive understanding of the importance of corporate culture, and an intuitive feeling for how to create a culture that people find motivating, inspiring, and rewarding.

Chapter 16

Yet Life Goes On

In a world of constant change and turmoil, running a complex business while also dealing with parenthood and the other demands of family life is a stressful challenge. Yet somehow, life goes on—mainly because there's really no good alternative.

Thankfully, I have a very close relationship with both of my children. I will take credit and say that that is absolutely by design. Even before Darryl and I began having kids, I was resolute about the type of family that I wanted to have—one based on mutual respect, honesty, support, and love—and my husband and I worked (and still work) very hard to cultivate it. (My next book will be about parenting.) The challenge of leading a family business during the period of COVID-19 strained those ties. But we found ways to keep them intact and, sometimes, even to make them a little stronger.

I'm thinking back to June 2020, about four months into the pandemic. Our daughter Ruby was a senior in high school, which meant she celebrated her graduation amidst the nuttiness of a pandemic. She and her classmates didn't have the chances most kids enjoy—to have a carefree prom, commencement ceremony, parties, and farewell gatherings. Of course, the pride of successfully completing high school and the excitement of starting a new phase of life were still very real for them. But graduating in a COVID-19 world was at best a bittersweet experience, and I felt sad for Ruby and her friends about that.

Of course, while Ruby was dealing with that, I was dealing with running Premier, the challenge of keeping it alive, and the emotional distress I experienced through having furloughed so many of our people. I definitely wasn't as present for Ruby as I normally would have been during this important time in her life. In fact, if I had to describe life under COVID-19 in one sentence, it would be, "I have never been home so much, yet seen my family so little."

However, in retrospect, the indescribable stress, volatility, and vulnerability that we all experienced added another layer to the relationship that I have with my kids and my husband. Through all the many moments of hysteria, grief, anxiety, and nausea, I didn't realize that I was having teachable moments—but I was.

My kids had the privilege (and, yes, I choose this word very carefully) of "seeing life." They had the opportunity to witness their parents as their truest selves, at their worst and at their best—navigating their lives and careers, coping with the impact that their decisions were having on other people. They were able to observe the depth and breadth of the reasoning, the emotion, and the self-questioning that go into life-altering decisions. And they were able to witness what it means to overcome adversity and make good things happen in the midst of darkness and tragedy.

Perhaps most important, they were able to see what a supportive marriage looks like. I would not have been able to survive the lockdown had it not been for my husband. (Without him, I either would have checked myself into some institution or just hidden out for months on end either at Canyon Ranch or at my favorite movie theatre—had either of them been open—ducking all my responsibilities and burrowing under the covers until the pandemic disappeared.)

One of the things that I truly value in our relationship is that, before I am about to share something important with my husband, I can tell him whether this is something that I want his advice on or not. "Or not" actually means "don't say anything at all." Basically, it means I just want him to listen, not to try to fix anything, not to tell me what to do, not even to comfort me—but just to be there. And when I ask for that, he does it—and he does it brilliantly.

Having said all this, for a period in June 2020, even with everything else in my life that demanded my attention, I definitely did focus on my daughter. Ruby was entering the next phase of her life—leaving the house, gaining new experiences, and creating her own memories. And to do this, she needed stuff! Pillows and sheets, bathrobes and laundry bins, socks and T-shirts, shelving and storage, toiletries and make-up, shoes and sandals and boots, and, and, and, and, and . . .

Which meant that Ruby and I had to spend time together in one of my Top Five Least Favorite Places to Go: The Mall.

This attitude of mine is a stark contrast to my eleven- and twelve-year-old self, who could not get enough of the mall—buying the must-have Lisa Frank stickers and eyeing the absolute coolest neon V-neck sweater that would be worn backwards to up the cool factor even more (a look that my friend Dana pulled off flawlessly).

Today, I hates the mall. Yet that is where I found myself heading with my daughter one very hot June day. As always, I was trying my best to follow the rule of not taking work calls while with my kids. But of course, on the drive to the mall I got a call. I had no intention of picking it up—until the number on the screen caught my eye.

The call was from Patrick. Patrick is indisputably the loveliest person that you will ever meet. Always happy, always calm, always with great perspective, always loving his family, always willing to help, always being the best guy that you could ever hang out with. I had basically grown up with Patrick, because he had been at Premier for over thirty years. He joined the company right out of college and eventually became a senior VP. He took me to my first meeting at our largest customer, where I started off so intimidated but where he quickly helped me become relaxed, fun, and productive. I learned immeasurable amounts from him. Patrick was the best.

In 2020, Patrick was nearing retirement. When COVID-19 hit, he suggested that this could be an ideal time for his exit. I was happy for Patrick but also heartbroken to be losing him. On this day, I had called Patrick earlier to thank him for his guidance, leadership, and generosity to me and to Premier over the many years. Now he was calling me back to return the verbal hug.

Patrick and I talked for several minutes as I sat with my daughter in the parking lot of the mall. When I got emotional, Ruby put her hand on my lap.

After I'd hung up, we got out of the car and headed toward the mall entrance. My eyes were still wet and my voice was still trembling. Ruby comforted me, saying, "Thanks for doing the right things during this crazy time."

How lucky am I?

(Ruby got an extra bathrobe that day, just for being so tremendous.)

I guess I must really be an amazing mother. Who else would allow their daughter to defer an Ivy League acceptance for two years in order to serve in the Israel Defense Forces? Sending my daughter off to a military career is not exactly what I'd dreamed about when I'd held her in my arms as a baby. But my kids actually blamed me for Ruby's decision, saying that I had inculcated them with values like service and sacrifice, and that they were just following my lead. Okay, guilty as charged.

Still, the timing couldn't have been worse. COVID-19 had a strong foothold the world over, and Israel, like most countries, had imposed strict rules on entry by foreigners, including a two-week period of quarantine. So in mid-2020, that is where Ruby and I found ourselves—in lockdown in a foreign country, albeit in an apartment in the city of Netanya with an amazing balcony and ocean view.

Those two weeks turned out to be absolutely exhausting. The seven-hour time difference between Israel and Philadelphia meant that I could actually work virtually twenty-four hours a day. We quickly settled into a routine. After waking up, my daughter and I took turns using my iPad to do workout videos on YouTube. After breakfast, Ruby began chatting with friends back home via phone and text message, while I started working via phone and Zoom. We came back together for lunch and dinner on the stunning balcony where we would chat, watch episodes of *Amy Schumer Learns to Cook*, and talk about Ruby's future. Saturdays were dedicated to games of Bananagrams and Rummikub. By the end of the two weeks, I think that we were tied in each.

In between these activities, we did our nails, napped, and baked goodies in the little kitchenette. (Actually, Ruby did all the baking. I just ate.) All while stuck in an apartment that we were forbidden to leave.

We also shared a series of major milestones: Ruby's birthday, her high school graduation, my birthday, my son's birthday, and Father's Day. All were celebrated in "the COVID way." Friends and family members had made special birthday videos for both Ruby and Maccabi. On Ruby's birthday, I decorated the balcony door with the number 18 made up of yellow Post-it notes, each inscribed with a few words naming something special about her. We watched Ruby's graduation on Zoom, eating cake and relishing the screams from the crowd as her father walked up to the podium to accept her diploma. I had balloons and candy delivered to Maccabi on his birthday, and a package of treats from Harry & David delivered to Darryl on Father's Day.

Finally, quarantine was over. We broke out and got to work, running around to every nearby store, mall, and pharmacy to ensure that Ruby had everything that she needed for her two years of service. We also threw in some sightseeing and a few dinners with friends. Those two weeks were even more exhausting than the quarantine.

As I was driving Ruby to her drop off, I asked her, "What was your favorite part of the trip?" Ruby picked one of the days we'd spent roaming around the city. Then she asked me the same question.

To my surprise, I found myself saying, "The time we spent in quarantine." Why? Because it was the most pure, uninterrupted, authentic time I've ever spent with my Ruby. What mother could ask for more?

Stowe, Vermont—within easy reach of Ben & Jerry's, the Trapp Family Lodge, a collection of great craft breweries, and enough mountain trails to provide days and days of great hikes. That is where my husband and I were in July 2021, enjoying our first real vacation in two years. We'd chosen Vermont because it is beautiful and drivable from Philadelphia. No flight meant no face masks. Before COVID-19, breathing used to be so underrated!

I certainly needed the time off. Leading Premier under pandemic conditions without a break was beginning to take its toll. So we'd have a solid week of mountain air, kayaking, great meals, and no work at all. That was the plan—until it wasn't.

Somehow, I found myself working—taking phone calls, participating in Zoom meetings, reading memos and reports, writing notes in the margins of spreadsheets, all in our beautiful hotel room while the natural beauty of Vermont beckoned from outside. But, to be honest, I didn't just "find myself working." I *chose* to work. The question is why?

Would Premier collapse in disarray over the course of a week? Would my key team members abandon the organization? Would our customers stop trusting us? I can say with 99.7 percent certainty that those things would not happen. Yet I acted as if they would. And I really didn't know why. Which is why, as I opened up yet another sales report, I would literally ask myself out loud—whether my husband was in the room or not—"Why am I doing this?"

It's funny—I am amazing at making plans. Work plans, travel plans, hang-out-with-friends plans, fun-kid-activity plans, you name it—I'm good at it and I enjoy it. But Julie's life plans? No dice. I seem to be incapable of thinking about my long-term future—including my life *after* work.

I know working people who dream about retiring someday. I don't. Do I even *want* to work less? I say that I eventually will, but I find that work energizes me more than anything else. I guess I like yoga, but how many yoga classes can I take? (Plus, I don't look great in yoga pants.) So imagining a life without work is basically impossible for me.

And I think that's why I choose to work all the time, even when I am theoretically on vacation with my husband. It's my way of fending off the mild case of panic I feel stirring inside me when I try to imagine a future without work. If I keep working, even when I shouldn't, it means I don't have to face the reality that, eventually, I will need to come up with some actual plan for life without work.

At the very least, I should come up with a hobby.

One night at dinner, I discussed it all with my husband. "Why am I working on vacation?" I asked. "I shouldn't be, right? I should just disconnect—turn off the phone, unplug the computer, stick the reports back in my bag and forget about it all for a week. That's what I should be doing, right?"

I expected my husband to agree—to say that I was right, that I did need to disconnect, that I should allow myself to let things go and refresh and restore my mind, body, and spirit.

But instead, he shook his head. "No, you should work," he said.

For a moment, I was taken aback. "What!" I demanded. "Don't you love and adore me infinitely? Isn't it unbearable to spend even a moment without me?"

He smiled. "Yes, I love you," he said. "But that's not it. You have an important job. There are things you need to do, no matter where you are and what day it is. You should do those things." He paused. "Of course, that doesn't mean you always have to do *every-thing*. That last call you took didn't sound very important. I think you could have skipped that one. But the one before that, you did need to do."

It's pretty special to have a husband who knows you even better than you do—and who accepts you exactly that way.

I guess the yoga classes will have to wait.

Perhaps most amazing of all, my relationship with my father has undergone a sea change in recent months.

It relates to my job as the 4G CEO of our family business—a job that's really about the evolution and sustainability of the company. Which decisions, which strategies, which initiatives will allow Premier to continue to thrive for decades to come? The responsibility, the privilege, and the challenge is to sustain and protect something that I was gifted with and that I am charged with passing along to the next generation of leaders.

I bet you know who Tom Brady is. (I understand he is a football megastar married to a model, though I don't know which team he plays for.) Anyway, I saw an amazing quote that he referred to "Never make a permanent decision based on a temporary emotion."

What a brilliant observation. And what a hard thing to do. It takes discipline, foresight, and balance, especially during times of turbulence and chaos. That is why I was so struck by it.

And this is where my huge level of respect for my father comes in. He led Premier out of a sense of legacy, out of undying love, respect, and appreciation for his father and grandfather. That was an enormous and selfless undertaking. I have been shaped in that essence, but I also bring my own edge to the task. What my father and I both feel is the immense pride and the huge obligation that we have to the business. This is not something that we verbally share—just an emotional understanding that binds us.

Recently, that binding force has become especially tangible.

We've been living through a time of serious threats to our business. My father and I tend to approach such threats in diametrically opposed ways—with different strategies, belief systems, and ways of acting. Sometimes I've responded to those differences with anger and frustration toward him. I know that my approach should sometimes be softer, and I am trying to do that more often—to really think before I engage.

And although I am still not aligned with my father in terms of preferred approaches, or sometimes even preferred outcomes, I've begun to feel that he is very much my ally, not an adversary or an obstacle. For the first time in my career at Premier, I am partnering with my father. I'm relating to him from a place of vulnerability and emoting, not out of anger or frustration, yet out of fear and lack of confidence—basically, as a daughter.

This is a new experience for me, and I am so grateful for it. As I am grateful to my father for receiving me in that way, for supporting me, for encouraging me, and for reassuring me.

The challenges of these hard times go on. Who knows? Maybe for Premier, and for countless other businesses around the world, the turmoil of recent years will become the new normal that we need to live with for decades to come. We'll see what the future brings. But as of now, as much as I hate having to manage through a period of constant crisis—and trust me when I say I fucking hate it—I am appreciative of what it has brought.

"Work/life balance," "Prioritize yourself." These are great coffee-cup slogans, but they don't correspond to much in the reality of a parent who is running a family business. Balance is ephemeral at best. And who can prioritize themselves in a world where emergencies are exploding around us on a daily basis—both on the TV news and in our personal inboxes and text message queues?

But that doesn't mean all is hopeless. If I was in the coffee-cup business, I'd just be switching to some other, more realistic slogans:

"Let your kids see who you really are."

"Feeling exhausted? Welcome to adulthood."

"Going shopping together is the ultimate form of love."

"When your work needs you, you need to work."

"Even family members deserve forgiveness."

And above all:

"Get over yourself."

Chapter 17

The Big Takeaways

*Thirteen Real-World Tips to Help You Run
Your Family Business Even Better*

As much as I hate to admit it, I don't know everything. Realizing this, I am sometimes scared to death that our family's hundred-plus year, four-generation legacy rests with me. I *cannot* be the one to fuck it up. This anxiety lives within me literally every day, every minute. During meetings: check; getting my nails done: check; at my son's lacrosse game: check. It is incessant.

But I am thankful for it. It drives me, and constantly reminds me that I always need to learn and improve.

Since becoming CEO of Premier, I have undertaken many changes. I've led a total organizational overhaul and a complete rebranding, made major investments in systems, hired people to support these new systems, and implemented an entirely new direction for the company. Not to mention handling the agonizing regulatory upgrades that have been mandated for medical device companies like ours.

Let me tell you, this shit ain't cheap! Cash wasn't exactly falling off the money tree. Thankfully, Premier—like most family businesses—is very financially conservative ("the dollar is round," you'll remember). So if you are a family business leader, or are hoping to become one, you need to be prepared to make some serious, maybe costly decisions—and then to take responsibility for the results, good or bad.

I'm hoping the experiences I've described in this book have given you some insights that will help you along the journey. What follows are some of the big takeaways I'd like to leave you with—my "I experiences"—as you close this book and look ahead to the next stage of your career adventure—whether you're a young person just starting out in business or a veteran leader with some scars and bruises from past battles.

1. Resentment Sucks

If you're lucky enough to be part of a family that runs a successful business, you may be tempted to join the business just because it's the path of least resistance. That's *not* a good reason to do it. Other *bad* reasons to join the family business are: because your parents keep pestering you to do so; because everyone has expected you to ever since you were a small child; because there's no one else in your generation who is willing or able to do it; or because you just can't think of any other career to pursue. Joining the family business is like any other career choice—you should do it only if you truly see it as a path to personal fulfillment, achievement, and growth.

What's more, as the stories I've told in this book illustrate, joining the family business is *not* an easy path to success. Yes, as a family member, you may enjoy some advantages that an "outsider" doesn't have. (It's easier to get an interview with the chairman of the board if he or she sits across from you at the dinner table every Sunday night.) But once you become part of the family business' leadership team, those advantages mean very little. Running a family business demands all the same skills, dedication, and integrity that are required to be successful in any business—plus the additional traits of humility, sensitivity, and emotional intelligence needed to navigate the tricky challenges that family dynamics almost always create.

So don't just drift into the family business because it's there, or because you can't think of anything better to do. If you do that, resentment will follow, and resentment sucks.

2. Exceed Even Your Own Expectations

Whenever a family member joins a family business, others in the company—as well as outsider partners, suppliers, and customers— probably assume that this person has received preferential treatment in hiring. (Guess what? They probably aren't wrong.) They may not say anything about it, but they may well be thinking it, consciously or unconsciously. This assumption may affect how people behave. If the family member makes a mistake on the job, even a small one, others may take it as "proof" that they are incompetent and got their job only through nepotism.

These attitudes may be unfair. But they're real, and basically unavoidable. The only way to minimize them is for you, the family member, to exceed *all* requirements and even your own expectations for your job. Listen, be quiet, ask questions, and work, work, work, work, work. Never take special advantage of company policies regarding vacation time, office locations, or other perks. Do everything you can to make it obvious that you have *earned* your place in the business, and are continuing to earn it, day in and day out.

3. Leave Your Family Baggage at the Door (as Best You Can)

We all know how emotionally fraught family relationships can be. Not everybody loves you. You don't love everybody. Deal with it.

Whatever the issue, you need to deal with it in a way that makes sense for you. Find outlets and supporters to help you, but make sure they are not people who are part of the family business. I'm all for shit-talking, but *never* about a family member with coworkers. Maybe this means working with a therapist to get those personal demons under control; talking with a counselor who can help you get past the worst of your resentments or jealousies; maybe even having a heart-to-heart talk with the person who you are in conflict with—outside of office hours, of course. Or it may just mean finding a good friend or a supportive spouse you can vent to. I have found my Young Presidents' Organization forum to be life changing—a space where I can talk about family business problems with peers who understand it all.

Whatever your personal method is, the key is to manage your family-bound emotions so they don't flare up in the workplace. We all find it delicious to watch family conflicts get acted out in business on a show like *Succession*. But when it happens in real life, it's a mess—bad for the people involved and bad for the business.

And yes, as you know from this book, I am not necessarily an ideal illustration of how to avoid this problem! But I am working on it (for reals—I love therapy).

4. Don't Be Intimidated by What You Don't Know

When you join any existing business, including a family business, you may find yourself surrounded by people with a lot more experience than you—people who may seem to know things about the business that feels like you have no hope of knowing. Makes sense. But it can also be intimidating. It can make you feel like an idiot when you are in meetings with these people. It can discourage you from offering your own ideas. In short, it can prevent you from thinking and acting like a leader. Don't let it.

If you are working with people who have deep knowledge of your industry, that's great. It creates a huge opportunity for you to learn. But if you're going to take advantage of that opportunity, you have to overcome your trepidation. Here's how:

First, do your homework. Read whatever you can find about the technical or business aspects of your industry. Watch videos, attend seminars, visit websites, subscribe to industry magazines. Little by little, you'll pick up the jargon and be able to start participating—intelligently—in meetings.

Second, ask questions. When you don't understand something that's being discussed, pipe up. Request a brief explanation. (You may not be the only one who could use it.) If you're too shy to ask for help the first time you need it, you may miss your best chance of getting it, since it will only make you feel much worse to ask the tenth time the topic is discussed.

Third, take advantage of the education that's available to you as a member of the family. In most companies, most people's jobs are siloed. Being in the family allows you to be exposed more broadly. This experience will be important to call on as you lead—remembering, relating, and requesting buy-in. People will be looking at you differently. You need to harness what you've picked up to make connections throughout the company and win people's support for your leadership.

Fourth, keep learning. Even after you develop some expertise in your industry, there will always be more to absorb, especially since, in today's world, change is constant. I've been with Premier for decades now, and I still often find myself in the same room with PhDs who know terms and equations I'll never understand. That's okay—I've learned that what matters most in business is *not* how many facts you can recite, but your ability to ask smart questions and then make good use of the answers.

I had the amazing opportunity to travel to South Africa and Australia for business. I knew I needed to prepare beforehand. I would be meeting with our dealers, as well as with dentists and hygienists and their study clubs. Reminder, I'm not a dentist nor a scientist. How in the actual fuck would I be able to teach them about our products, our technologies, and the supporting science?

Answer: I studied *hard*. I spent a lot of time with our head of R&D, who was an amazing teacher and had the ability to break everything down into colloquialisms that I could understand. I took these learnings and a ridiculously strong fake-it-'til-you-make-it attitude and presented successfully to these various groups. Next time you see me, ask me to tell you about how Premier's varnish with ACP is like taking American cheese and turning it into Swiss cheese—and why that's important.

As I do at all of my presentations, I encouraged questions. One I was asked many times during this trip was, "You're not a dentist!?"

5. Before You Hire, Think Once, Twice, Three Times

As a leader in any business—family business or otherwise—one of your most important responsibilities is hiring the right people. It's also one of the hardest. If you've ever played a leadership role, you've probably had an experience like this: You hire someone who seems really impressive for a key position; you communicate your expectations about the job to them; everyone is excited about the new team member. For a short time, everything is rosy. But then, somehow, it all stops working. Their deliverables aren't the right deliverables, their sense of what is needed is off, the vibe is wrong. The new hire begins to become bothersome rather than influential and integral.

What happened?

It's actually what *didn't* happen. From the outset, before the person was even hired, as the job description was being crafted and as the list of required skills was being refined, you were missing key elements. Your vision of the job was shortsighted, there were functions that weren't fully considered, or there were reporting re-lationships that weren't quite clear. When you fail to concretize and communicate your vision for a position in a deep, thoughtful, prag-matic, and expansive way, the person you hire—no matter how tal-ented—will not be able to do the job that you wanted, or thought you wanted. Ultimately, they will have to be terminated. The whole process leads to a loss of time, money, morale, and momentum.

To use the old cliché from relationship breakups, "The problem isn't you, it's me." That is, I made a mistake by bringing you on to fill a job that was unclear, poorly structured, maybe even unnecessary. This is one of the most painful lessons I had to learn as a leader. The scribbled org charts I create when designing a new role now have much more detail. I've learned to *really* think through what I am doing before I make any hiring move. The results are much better.

6. Forget About Work/Life Balance

It's ironic: "Family business" does *not* necessarily mean "family-friendly." Being part of a family business doesn't mean that you will escape the universal problem of figuring out how to lead an organization while also finding time to be a responsible, caring, and deeply engaged spouse, parent, or family member in general.

It's a problem that has generated thousands of newspaper and magazine articles, TV and radio segments, podcasts, books, and seminars. The bad news is that it is a problem with no solution. The truth is that if you are truly committed to leading a business—family business or not—you are going to have to dedicate a level of time and energy to the job that makes deep personal connections incredibly difficult to maintain. There *will* be evenings spent at the office rather than having dinner with the family, weekends of poring over spreadsheets and reports rather than enjoying family outings, school concerts and plays that you will miss, romantic dinners with your significant other that will get postponed, family holidays that will get cut short. This is the reality you will grapple with, and the sooner you realize it, the better.

Is it possible to live this way while still feeling happy and fulfilled? That's a question every individual has to answer for themselves. I think the answer is yes, provided you love your business and the work required to make it successful; provided you have a spouse, children, and other family members who understand your commitment and are willing to support you in it; and provided you are well organized enough so that you are able to break away from work at least once in a while to reconnect with those you love. Lots of "provideds," but that's the truth.

As for work/life balance—it doesn't exist. For a business leader, in any given week, month, or year, it's likely that work will dominate your calendar and your mind. What you may be able to achieve, however, is some degree of work/life *acceptance*. There may be one or more periods in your life when you shift gears and devote your energy to activities outside of work—philanthropy, social causes, creative endeavors, personal growth, spirituality, and, yes, family bonding. These periods might take the form of preplanned sabbaticals, retreats, breaks, or post-career shifts. You can look to other business leaders whom you know and admire for examples of how they've planned and carried out these sorts of life changes.

On a day-to-day basis, it's very unlikely you'll achieve work/life balance. But hopefully, you'll be able to feel that you're giving the best of yourself to *all* the things, in whatever proportion, that make life meaningful for you.

I'm still getting there. Case in point: I'm working on this book chapter at 8 PM on a Tuesday night when I should be studying to get my scuba certification, which I promised my son I would do!

I'll get there.

7. Change Is Your Friend

Leading a business is about coping with change—especially in today's world, in which technology, customer needs, competition, and economic conditions are constantly and unpredictably on the move. That means business as usual is *not* a formula for future success, even if you run a business that has enjoyed profitable growth for decades or generations.

But modifying what you're accustomed to doing is never easy. People tend to have an ingrained emotional resistance to change. When you work in a business with a proud tradition of success, it's easy for your team members to convince themselves that the way we've always done things is the best. People may shut down their willingness to look at innovative processes or concepts pioneered by other businesses, justifying themselves by saying, "Our industry is so unique that we have nothing to learn from other companies." This attitude is so common in business that it has been given a name, the "not-invented-here syndrome." And family businesses can be especially prone to it—after all, challenging traditions is even more emotionally difficult when it implies criticizing things your parents or grandparents did.

As a family business leader, you need to find ways to forge a culture that is open to change. Make innovation part of everyone's job description; provide financial rewards and public praise for people who produce new ideas that create value for your business and its customers. Create opportunities for your team members to learn from outsiders—for example, by scheduling visits from experts from companies in different but related industries and by looking for opportunities to partner with outside firms that have capabilities your own business lacks. You may even want to set up an internal innovation unit or "skunkworks" to experiment with new products, processes, and business models.

Above all, remember that change isn't the enemy—it's your friend.

8. Surround Yourself with Truth-Tellers

Another problem that family business leaders have is figuring out what is *really* going on in and around your business. This is a challenge for leaders in every kind of business—but it is probably worse in a family business. A family has a communications network of its own—a kind of grapevine that exists outside of and separate from the business, that only family members can access. You have connections with other members of the family on evenings, weekends, and holidays. You have the opportunity to talk about the business while on family road trips and during dinner parties. You don't need to wait for an official announcement or memo to learn about what your fellow family members are thinking—you have access to inside information that ordinary employees don't.

This is all good—but it can sometimes mean that you end up working inside a bubble, where you get most of your news about what is going on in the business from a handful of people. If you head up the company, you may find that you hear only good news from the people who report to you. And, of course, this problem will get worse if you develop the habit of responding negatively to bad news—with anger, blame, or denial.

To prevent this from happening, surround yourself with people who are self-confident and smart enough to tell you the truth, even when you may not like it. I actually say to my people, "Do I seem like someone who can't take what you are going to tell me? Tell me the truth—I can take it." The highest form of loyalty is *not* to pretend that the boss can do no wrong and not to shield them—it's to help the boss to see when she is heading down the wrong path, and to help her get back on track, for her own benefit and for the good of the company. People who practice that kind of loyalty are rare, and they are super valuable.

9. Think Two Steps Ahead

The most important job of a company leader is to see the big picture—the long-term trends that are shaping the company's future, and the steps you need to take to ensure that future will be long-lasting and successful. This skill isn't something that comes naturally to most people. It takes training, practice, and deliberate effort.

It's especially true if you have worked your way to the top of the organization after starting in some specific department or niche—the way I did at Premier. If you spent your first few years in the business focusing on one particular set of issues and challenges—product development, sales, customer service, marketing, financial management, or whatever—it's easy to retain that narrow lens even after you rise in the organization and take on much broader responsibilities.

So as your career progresses, pay conscious attention to the need to expand your horizons and learn to think strategically about the long-term future of your business. There are lots of ways you can practice this new skill. For me, earning my master's degree in business was an important way to hone this kind of thinking. But you may not need to take on a complete MBA program to get the same benefit—attending lectures and workshops, watching You-Tube videos (not kidding), and taking specific classes focused on business strategy, market analysis, emerging economic trends, and similar topics can also be extremely helpful. Read mind-opening books and articles by big thinkers in business, including not just the latest trendy bestsellers but classic books by gurus whose wisdom has stood the test of time.

Make connections with experts who can help you hone your strategic thinking skills—academics, veteran executives from your own or other industries, consultants with real insight into the ways the business world is evolving. Spend time with them brainstorming about possible future scenarios for your company. They can help you develop a big-picture understanding of your industry, and they can help you practice looking at your business as it might appear to outsiders—customers, suppliers, competitors.

Of course, it's not possible to predict the future with certainty. But with practice, you can develop the ability to see major developments in your industry as they are happening, rather than waiting for their impact to hit you. Then you can take the steps needed to prepare yourself and your people to address tomorrow's challenges today, which can help to ensure your company's enduring survival and success.

10. Sweat the Details

At the same time that the company leader needs to take a long view of the business's future, she also needs to pay close attention to the details that determine its short-term success. Balancing these two ends of the scale is one of the toughest challenges for a business leader. It's like learning to look through a telescope and a microscope at the same time—while being clear-eyed enough to combine the two perspectives in a single vision. Learning to do this takes constant practice. And yes, it can give you a headache, for sure.

Sweating the details means never assuming that any specific element of your business is too small for you to worry about. Little things can make or break a company, which means you need to pay attention to all of them. Tycoon John D. Rockefeller used to brag about how he noticed that assembly-line workers were using a few drops of extra solder when sealing drums of kerosene for shipment. He pointed out that they could cut costs and save time by eliminating the extra solder—which ended up saving the company a few thousand dollars every year. Petty? Yes, but multiply it by a thousand other details and you understand better how Rockefeller built Standard Oil into a world-dominating giant (and made himself the world's richest man in the process).

No matter how high you may rise in your organization, stay in touch with the details that affect its success. Listen in on some service calls to see how well your business is treating its customers. Visit the facilities where your products are made to get a feel for the efficiency of their operations. Ask tough questions about how quality standards are maintained.

Recognize the good work of the people who are executing in the small details and who take the time to show you how they do what they do. (I actually learned to drive the forklift in our warehouse the other day—Jesse is a great teacher!) When people at every level of a company know that the big boss pays attention to the details of their work, they end up doing a better job—because they know that the small decisions they make every day actually matter.

11. Be a Governor: Think Smart About Business Governance Issues

Thinking holistically about the future of the business isn't just about competitive strategy or market trends. It's also about the ownership and leadership structure of the company—who controls it, who benefits from it, how key decisions get made. Obviously, the specifics of business governance are complicated matters with complex legal and financial implications. You'll want and need professional help to sort out how they should be handled in your particular company. There are lawyers, accountants, bankers, and others with the background needed to support your decision-making process, including professionals with extensive history in dealing with family businesses. Their help can be life-saving.

Having said that, here are five tips I would personally offer to you as you begin dealing with these important governance issues as they relate to your family business:

1. **The business will employ a law firm to manage the entire process—but you should also engage a lawyer to advise you personally and to represent your individual interests.** This is a family affair, but what's best for you and what's best for other members of the family may not always be perfectly aligned. When all parties have advice and representation to defend their interests, then the chances for creating a plan that is fair to everyone are greatly enhanced.

2. **Be respectful of everyone involved in the process—difficult as this may be at times.** Big decisions about the future of a family business involve money, power, prestige,

and pride—all matters that generate strong emotional re-actions. No matter how much all the family members love one another, the discussions are likely to become conten-tious. Work hard to avoid saying or doing things that you may later regret or that may end up burning bridges among family members. If you keep your head, even when others may lose theirs, in the end you'll be glad you did. Trust me, I've been "headless" myself—it's not cute.

3. **Be communicative.** You can only get what you ask for—so don't assume the other members of the family, or the professional advisors and representatives involved in the process, understand what you need, want, and value. Speak clearly about what matters to you and about the kind of arrangements that you consider fair and beneficial to the business—and when necessary, repeat yourself until you are sure you have been heard.

4. **Bring data to the table.** As with any negotiating process, you will achieve more if you know as much as you can. This means understanding the family, its philosophies and preferences; the strengths, weaknesses, and needs of the business as it faces a challenging future; the kinds of ar-rangements that other families have made when faced with similar business issues; and so on. If you do your home-work and shape your ideas according to what you learn, you'll be more likely to end up with an agreement that allows for a solid future.

5. **Plan for the non-end.** Although it's difficult, you need to balance current interests with the needs of future genera-tions. Strive to leave them a business and a dynamic that will raise as few questions and difficulties as possible.

12. Remember That You Are Also a Person

Yes, as a CEO you are a leader, a champion, and, if you're doing the job right, a visionary. From the moment I accepted this role at Premier, I knew all this. But I never realized that, to my team, I am also a person. It's a reality that struck me recently through one of the most impactful experiences I've ever had.

Leanne was a long-time sales rep who worked one of Premier's territories. Lee was fabulous, one of those people that you always want to be around—gregarious, carefree, and fun. I didn't get to see Lee very often, but when I did, she just picked me up. (Mind you, this is hard to do—my baseline is generally very high!) Leanne had seen me evolve, grow, and ultimately rise to the role of CEO. She was very proud of me. She loved calling me "Boss Bitch," always told me what a great job I was doing, and never failed to notice a new piece of jewelry I was wearing.

So when I heard that Leanne was diagnosed with stage IV cancer, I was overcome.

I called her right away just to let her know that I was thinking of her. She didn't pick up her phone—I hadn't expected her to—so I left her as upbeat and encouraging a message as I could.

A few weeks later, Lite, her immediate boss, told me that Lee would be entering hospice. When he told me, I took a few quiet minutes to myself, just to think of Lee, smile for her, and cry a bit. She would be with her family for her remaining time, so I figured that would be my goodbye.

So I was thunderstruck when, a day or two later, Lee's brother called and said that Lee wanted to talk to me. Of course, I would love to talk to her. But I was astounded that that is what she wanted.

Through Lee's brother, we scheduled a call for the next day.

I was extremely nervous. I had never had a conversation like this before. Would it be a lucid call? What should I say? How should the conversation end?

In search of guidance, I called a very close friend who had lost her father, way too early, after a long illness. She helped me organize my thoughts. She advised me to just listen, to tell her how much she meant to me, and recall some times that we'd shared together.

I made the call at the designated time, and Lee was Lee. She sounded fantastic, just like her usual self. She asked about my kids, remembering specific details, and asked me about things going on at work. It was stunning—Lee was literally on her deathbed, and here she was asking how *I* was doing!

Our relationship was so close that I felt able to be very straightforward with Lee. I said, "I think you should be selfish. Let's focus the conversation on you."

In response, Lee told me that she'd had a great life—the life she wanted—and that she was thrilled to have spent so much of it with Premier. She was especially appreciative that she'd been able to work with three generations of Charlesteins—my grandfather, my father, and me.

Blown away can't begin to describe how I felt. How could my family have made such an impact on her? After all, at the end of the day, her work with Premier was a job. Except it was more than that to Lee. We'd been an integral, important, and meaningful part of her life. How humbling. This is something that I never could have realized without her.

When Lee asked about how Premier's sales were going, I gave her a couple of details, then told her, "I'm going to dedicate this sales year to you."

"Oh, you can't do that," she protested.

"Remember, I'm the boss," I told her. "I'm in charge, and I can do whatever I want." She loved that!

I thanked Lee for being in my life and for always bolstering me. And I ended the call by asking whether I could arrange for another call with her. That's where we left things—although, sadly, that was the last time we spoke.

Don't wait for a sad moment like this one to realize the importance of your human connections with the people you work with. Understand this from day one, and let it help guide the way you treat those you come into contact with.

13. Be Authentic

Running a family business is an awesome responsibility. Choices you make will affect the lives of countless people—customers, suppliers, partners, employees, their family members, and, of course, your own family members who have entrusted you with the future of the company.

There will be times when you will feel a little overwhelmed by the job. Making business decisions in circumstances that are complicated, confusing, multifaceted, and ever changing is difficult at best. Sometimes you will feel completely inadequate.

When this happens, you may be tempted to stop being yourself. You may think you are expected to play a role, to pretend to be someone you're not—the image of the ideal business leader, with gravitas, toughness, profound wisdom, limitless knowledge, eloquence, and charisma, like someone on the cover of *Fortune* magazine. Rather than the person you really are—nervous, insecure, uncertain, tongue-tied, scared.

I get that. I've had all those feelings. Sometimes I still do.

But what I've come to learn is that you're always better off being who you really are, with all your strengths, vulnerabilities, and weaknesses. The people around you—including most of the people you fear may judge you—actually appreciate it when you show your true self. They understand that it takes grit and self-confidence to be transparent and real. And when you are willing to show your own uncertainties and struggles, it empowers them to do the same. Which means that the business challenges you all face can be put on the table openly, for the entire team to tackle and solve together.

I've tried to model this value of authenticity in the pages of this book. Having read this far, you know I am nobody's idea of a picture-perfect, magazine-cover CEO. But so far, being who I am has worked for me and for Premier. I plan to keep going this way for as long as I can.

Acknowledgments

I am forever indebted to the people of Premier. Those who began in 1913, the generations thereafter, and those who are working at our outstanding organization today. This story, my growth, stands on your shoulders. You are my teachers, my friends, and my purpose. To Karl Weber, my writing partner, who, for whatever unfortunate (for him) reason, was stuck with me. A star at bringing guidance, humor, and calm to a first-time book author. To John Willig, an agent with a smile. To Matt, Katie, Alyn, Brigid, and the whole BenBella Team—just amaze-balls people who decided to take a chance on me. To David Hahn, a quiet and unassuming driver. To my Forum, past and present, whose guidance, experiences, and support have shaped me. And to Gil Bashe, my instant friend and mentor, Renaissance man, and cheerleader.

Julie Charlestein
Philadelphia, Pennsylvania
June 2022

About the Author

Julie Charlestein is a Philadelphia-based business leader and health-care innovator who serves as the CEO of Premier Dental, a global provider of inspired solutions for daily dentistry. Leading a century-old business as the company's fourth-generation chief executive, Julie is recognized within the dental industry and beyond as a champion of creative health-care solutions to meet the evolving needs of today's patients.

She was voted one of the Top 25 Most Influential Women in Dentistry by *Dental Products Report* and recognized as one of *Philadelphia Business Journal*'s "Most Admired CEOs." Julie was awarded the Silver Stevie Award as Female Executive of the Year, honored with the Gold Award by the Best in Biz Awards as Executive of the Year, and nominated as one of IFAH's Top 100 Health-care Leaders. The *Wall Street Journal* featured her perspective in the WSJ-Pro AI cover story "AI Helps Medical Device Makers Punch Above Their Weight."

She currently serves on the Board of Overseers for the University of Pennsylvania School of Dental Medicine, the Dean's Advisory Council of Temple University Dental School, and the Board of ASDOH (Arizona School of Dentistry and Oral Health).

She has previously served on the Dean's Advisory Board of the School of Dental Medicine at Harvard University. Julie has served as the Chair of the Government Relations Committee for the Dental Trade Alliance and is a member of the Young Presidents' Organization (YPO). She holds a bachelor's degree from Emory University and a master's degree from Temple University.

Julie is also the founder and visionary of izzo®, a direct-to-consumer e-commerce company. izzo® is the first and only professionally inspired 4-in-1 oral care system, and can be found at www.izzosmile.com.

Julie lives in the suburbs of Philadelphia with her delicious family.